The Hamlyn
CURRY
Cookbook

The Hamlyn
CURRY
Cookbook
Meera Taneja

Hamlyn
London · New York · Sydney · Toronto

To my dearest parents,
Madanlal and Satya Khosla, with love

The following titles are also available in this series:
Barbecue Cookbook · Chicken Cookbook
Cocktails and Mixed Drinks · Contact Grill
Cooking for Two · The Diabetic Cookbook
Egg and Cheese Cookbook · Fred's Pastry Book
Hamlyn Pressure Cookbook · Kitchen Magic
Mighty Mince Cookbook · No need to Cook Book
Woman and Home Favourite Recipes

Cover photography by Paul Williams
Photography by Paul Williams
Illustrations by Sally Launder

Published by The Hamlyn Publishing Group Limited
London · New York · Sydney · Toronto
Astronaut House, Feltham, Middlesex, England
© Copyright The Hamlyn Publishing Group Limited 1982

Reprinted 1983

ISBN 0 600 32272 6

Set in 10 on 11pt Apollo by Photocomp Limited, Birmingham, England
Printed in Italy

Contents

Useful facts and figures

Notes on metrication

In this book quantities are given in metric and Imperial measures. Exact conversion from Imperial to metric measure does not usually give very convenient working quantities and so the metric measures have been rounded off into units of 25 grams. The table below shows the recommended equivalents.

Ounces	Approx. g to nearest whole figure	Recommended conversion to nearest unit of 25	Ounces	Approx. g to nearest whole figure	Recommended conversion to nearest unit of 25
1	28	25	11	312	300
2	57	50	12	340	350
3	85	75	13	368	375
4	113	100	14	396	400
5	142	150	15	425	425
6	170	175	16 (1 lb)	454	450
7	198	200	17	482	475
8	227	225	18	510	500
9	255	250	19	539	550
10	283	275	20 (1¼ lb)	567	575

Note: When converting quantities over 20 oz first add the appropriate figures in the centre column, then adjust to the nearest unit of 25. As a general guide, 1 kg (1000 g) equals 2·2 lb or about 2 lb 3 oz. This method of conversion gives good results in nearly all cases, although in certain pastry and cake recipes a more accurate conversion is necessary to produce a balanced recipe.

Liquid measures The millilitre has been used in this book and the following table gives a few examples.

Imperial	Approx. ml to nearest whole figure	Recommended ml	Imperial	Approx. ml to nearest whole figure	Recommended ml
¼ pint	142	150 ml	1 pint	567	600 ml
½ pint	283	300 ml	1½ pints	851	900 ml
¾ pint	425	450 ml	1¾ pints	992	1000 ml (1 litre)

Spoon measures All spoon measures given in this book are level unless otherwise stated.

Can sizes At present, cans are marked with the exact (usually to the nearest whole number) metric equivalent of the Imperial weight of the contents, so we have followed this practice when giving can sizes.

Oven temperatures The table below gives recommended equivalents.

	°C	°F	Gas Mark		°C	°F	Gas Mark
Very cool	110	225	$\frac{1}{4}$	Moderately hot	190	375	5
	120	250	$\frac{1}{2}$		200	400	6
Cool	140	275	1	Hot	220	425	7
	150	300	2		230	450	8
Moderate	160	325	3	Very hot	240	475	9
	180	350	4				

Notes for American and Australian users

Note: American terms and measures are shown in brackets throughout the recipes.

In America the 8-oz measuring cup is used. In Australia metric measures are now used in conjunction with the standard 250-ml measuring cup. The Imperial pint, used in Britain and Australia, is 20 fl oz, while the American pint is 16 fl oz. It is important to remember that the Australian tablespoon differs from both the British and American tablespoons; the table below gives a comparison. The British standard tablespoon, which has been used throughout this book, holds 17·7 ml, the American 14·2 ml, and the Australian 20 ml. A teaspoon holds approximately 5 ml in all three countries.

British	American	Australian
1 teaspoon	1 teaspoon	1 teaspoon
1 tablespoon	1 tablespoon	1 tablespoon
2 tablespoons	3 tablespoons	2 tablespoons
$3\frac{1}{2}$ tablespoons	4 tablespoons	3 tablespoons
4 tablespoons	5 tablespoons	$3\frac{1}{2}$ tablespoons

An Imperial/American guide to solid and liquid measures

Imperial	American	Imperial	American
SOLID MEASURES		LIQUID MEASURES	
1 lb butter or	1 lb butter or	$\frac{1}{4}$ pint liquid	$\frac{2}{3}$ cup liquid
margarine	2 cups	$\frac{1}{2}$ pint	$1\frac{1}{4}$ cups
1 lb flour	4 cups	$\frac{3}{4}$ pint	2 cups
1 lb granulated or		1 pint	$2\frac{1}{2}$ cups
caster sugar	2 cups	$1\frac{1}{2}$ pints	$3\frac{3}{4}$ cups
1 lb icing sugar	3 cups	2 pints	5 cups
8 oz rice	1 cup		($2\frac{1}{2}$ pints)

NOTE: When making any of the recipes in this book, only follow one set of measures as they are not interchangeable.

Introduction

Why, I wonder, is it so often assumed that a curry must come from India? With the spread of its popularity across the world curry is a dish of universal appeal, and could, in fact, come from any part of Asia or the Caribbean. The literal translation of the word 'curry' – or 'Kari' – is 'sauce' and though, strictly speaking, anything cooked in a sauce could be labelled 'curry', the term is chiefly associated with Asian – and especially Indian – cooking.

In the course of the last few centuries traders and emigrant workers from India travelled widely, settling as far afield as South East Asia, Sri Lanka, East Africa and the Caribbean. And with them they took the essential herbs and spices that made up their aromatic and spicy food. Today you are as likely to find a curry in Trinidad as you are in Madras, though it will differ considerably in character and flavour. Each area has developed its own piquancy, making full use of local ingredients as well as the traditional ones that have been imported. In time, I am sure even a British curry will evolve.

The characteristics of the curries from different parts of the world depend entirely on the variety and balance of the herbs and spices that go into their creation. It is fascinating to see how it is possible to trace the use of certain spices in some areas to their country of origin. When the people from East India, for example, settled in Trinidad the spices that they took with them were similar to those used in eastern Indian cooking to this day – seeds of fenugreek, fennel, cumin, nigella, coriander and turmeric. But with the introduction over the years of local spices and other ingredients such as coconut milk, wine and rum, the present-day curries of Trinidad, Martinique and other Caribbean islands bear little resemblance to the original recipes brought from India by the early immigrants all those years ago.

Local influence plays a great part in distinguishing curries from different areas. Those from North and East India and indeed any with a strong Mughlai influence will be of a pleasant deep yellow or rust colour, but those from South India, where there is widespread use of grated coconut and coconut milk, have a whitish appearance. In Sri Lanka the curries are often very dark in colour, due to the custom of dry roasting the spices before grinding them. Virtually no Sri Lankan or South East Asian dish is complete without the addition of blachan, the shrimp paste, powder or sauce used to enhance the flavour. Other local additions are lemon grass, rampe leaves, loas and the various types of nut – modifications to the original curry recipes introduced by immigrants from South India who came to work on the rubber plantations of Malaya. The cuisine of South India is very distinct from the rest of India, and these immigrants brought with them the herbs and spices they most commonly used – curry leaves, mustard seeds, tamarind, coconut and coriander.

During the years of British rule people from Punjab in North India and Gujaratis from West India emigrated to East Africa. Many Indians still live there and have taken on East African nationality, but very little native influence has found its way into their cooking, and the original Indian recipes have remained largely unchanged. Strange that the people of two distinct cultures, living alongside each other for a considerable length of time, have not exchanged or incorporated into their diets any of the more interesting features of each other's cuisine.

But from whatever part of the world a curry comes, its special characteristics and delicacy of flavour will depend on the careful selection and blending of the individual herbs and spices. No commercially produced curry powder will produce a perfect result. Certain spices are either dry or oil roasted, ground and stored for later use, but these alone will not complete the delicate spicing that is required to produce a really good curry. Whether the curry should be hot enough to bring tears to your eyes or just mild or even totally bland without the addition of any chillies is a matter entirely for your personal taste.

A 'warm' curry is produced by using spices such as cloves, green and black cardamoms, cinnamon, bay leaves, mace, black pepper and nutmeg. Ground together, these spices make what is known in Indian cooking as 'garam masala' – literally, 'warm combination of spices'. This blend of spices is most often used in the preparation of non-vegetarian dishes all over India. Although they are grown in the south, they are more widely used in the north where the climate is more extreme in the winter. Chillies are the ingredients that create a 'hot' curry, inducing a burning sensation which helps you to perspire and which consequently has a refreshing cooling effect in very hot climates.

As an accompaniment to curry, rice is a universal favourite, often flavoured with cloves or other spices according to regional custom. Various breads such as chapati, poori and parathas may also be served, or dall – beans or other pulses – together with a host of side dishes comprising pickles, chutneys, sambals and salads. Even the simplest Asian meal will consist of three or four main dishes of vegetables, meat or poultry, with a wide choice of side dishes. A traditional meal combines the separate courses of a European meal into one, often finishing simply with a choice of fresh fruits, light and refreshing. Desserts and sweetmeats are more often eaten at teatime or as between-meals snacks.

Spices are the essential ingredients used both to flavour and enhance the colour of curries. Most supermarkets offer a wide range of spices and any unusual ingredients can be purchased from Indian stores or wholefood shops. They should be treated with respect and purchased in small quantities as they lose their essential oils and flavour if they are stored for too long. Even if kept in airtight containers in a dry place, they should not be kept indefinitely and are best stored whole and ground in small quantities as they are required. Freshly ground spices have a stronger flavour than when they have been stored and should be used carefully. When whole spices are used they may be wrapped in a small piece of muslin and removed when the dish is served – it depends on individual tastes; I like to bite into a clove or cardamom as I eat a curry.

To prepare an authentic curry, no special equipment is needed. A pestle and mortar are the best tools for grinding spices as the slow pounding releases all the natural oils; or a metal pepper mill may be used for this purpose. An electric coffee grinder may also be used but it should be set aside specifically for grinding spices. Similarly, a liquidiser or food processor will effectively grind larger quantities of spices but they may permanently discolour or taint the vessel. A word of warning – never try to grind turmeric root, dried root ginger or large pieces of fresh root ginger in an electric grinder or liquidiser as they are too tough and may break the blades. A wok is a useful addition to your kitchen utensils: it is more efficient than a frying pan for stir-frying and uses less oil. But your best ally is patience.

To appreciate the true art of both cooking and eating curries, one has to remember that it simply cannot be hurried along. Remember that the Asian housewife is happy to spend many hours preparing food for her household. Meal time, in the Asian world, is a very relaxed affair, and the womenfolk often join their hostess in helping to prepare the food so that it becomes an enjoyable social event rather than a chore.

I have chosen the recipes in this book in the hope that you will enjoy the experience of cooking and eating them as much as I have in testing them. As you travel across the world with me, sampling the delights of curry cooking according to the tastes and customs of different regions, it is my hope that you, too, will come to appreciate the art, and discover the pleasure to be derived from the creation of a superb curry. When you become familiar with the recipes you will be able to vary the quantities and proportions of the spices according to your own preference, for this, after all, is the purpose of all good cooking – to find the balance of flavours which will give you the most pleasure. And to this end, in true Eastern style, my best wishes go to all you would-be curry cooks.

Meera Taneja

India

India – that vast land of ancient culture, mystery and charm – is a gourmet's paradise and the source of culinary wealth as diverse as its many peoples. It is as the home of curry for which India is renowned, and therefore fitting that my curry-eating journey should begin there.

From the beautiful state of Kashmir in the North with its high-capped Himalayan mountains and lush green valley come dishes rich with the use of ghee – clarified butter – thickened with ground fennel seeds and yogurt. The fertile plains of the Punjab with its five rivers produce the wide variety of pulses that comprises so much of the rich, aromatic food of this region and from here comes the Tandoor – the unglazed clay oven which has given its name to a particular style of cooking, now familiar in the West.

The fried delicacies and vegetarian dishes of Central India are a happy combination of their mixed Hindu and Muslim heritage, while the strong vegetarian tradition of the western state of Gujarat provides some of the most delicious recipes, highly spiced and hot, simple but inventive. Fish dishes from the Maharashtrans, egg specialities from the Parsees and the chilli-hot vindaloos, favourites of the Goans, are some of the other delights universally appreciated.

Many of the dishes from the South are unique to a particular area and the food is very rich, highly spiced and hot with chillies. Coconuts and rice are extensively used and in the East, too, rice is the staple diet. Mouth-watering fish and seafood recipes abound from this region, and from here come the famous sweetmeats made from milk and soft cheese.

Travelling through India from north to south or east to west is a unique culinary experience and being almost too fond of good food, whenever I visit India I find it hard to avoid indulging in sheer gluttony. I hope, however, that in the following pages by introducing a brief sample of some of the dishes from the various regions it may be possible to give you a taste of the pleasures such a journey provides.

North India

Murghi Bade Sabha
Chicken with almonds in spicy sauce

(Illustrated on front cover)
I find chicken one of the most versatile ingredients. It can be cooked in a variety
of ways and used in endless interesting dishes. This chicken is simmered gently
in its own juice with tomatoes, onions and yogurt. No additional stock or water
is required as the natural juices make enough sauce on their own.
Chapatis (page 122) or Naan (page 123) should be served with this dish.

SERVES 4 · PREPARATION TIME 20 MINUTES · COOKING TIME 1¼ HOURS

1 (1·25-kg/2½-lb) chicken
450 g/1 lb onions
2·5-cm/1-in piece fresh root ginger
1 green chilli (chili pepper) – optional
2 cloves garlic
1 teaspoon ground cumin
2 bay leaves
6 whole cloves
4 green cardamons
6 black peppercorns
2·5-cm/1-in stick cinnamon

2 teaspoons ground fennel seeds
1 teaspoon chilli powder
½ teaspoon turmeric
salt to taste
1 teaspoon dried mint
3 tablespoons natural yogurt
225 g/8 oz (½ lb) ripe tomatoes
75 g/3 oz (6 tablespoons) ghee
1 tablespoon chopped coriander leaves
50 g/2 oz (½ cup) slivered almonds,
    lightly toasted

Skin the chicken and cut it into eight portions. Roughly chop the onions, ginger and the green chilli if used. Finely chop or crush the garlic. Mix the ingredients together and spoon a layer of them into the bottom of a heavy-based saucepan. Arrange the chicken pieces on top, then sprinkle on all the spices, the salt and mint. Cover with a tight-fitting lid, place over low heat and leave to cook very gently for 15–20 minutes until the onions and chicken have released their own cooking liquid. Stir the mixture thoroughly to combine all the ingredients then stir in the natural yogurt. Re-cover the pan and continue to cook gently for another 15 minutes. Meanwhile, chop the tomatoes and add to the chicken together with the ghee. Stirring frequently, cook the mixture until the tomatoes are reduced to a pulp. Cover closely and cook very gently for 25–30 minutes until the chicken is tender and the sauce thickens.

Serve hot, sprinkled with chopped coriander leaves and the lightly toasted slivered almonds.

Rogan Josh
Spiced lamb in yogurt

*Kashmir, the northernmost state of India, is a land of breathtaking landscapes,
beautiful women and a rich mixture of Hindu and Muslim cooking traditions.
Rogan Josh, a world-famous dish from this region, is unique in its subtle use of
spices, with special emphasis on aniseed which is not normally found in savoury
dishes in any other region of India. No onions are used to thicken the dish as the
spices themselves are the thickening agents.
Serve with plain boiled rice.*

SERVES 4–6 · PREPARATION TIME 15 MINUTES · COOKING TIME 1 HOUR

1 kg/2¼ lb tender boneless lamb
4 tablespoons mustard oil
4 cloves
small pinch of asafoetida
600 ml/1 pint (2½ cups) natural yogurt
2 teaspoons chilli powder

salt to taste
3 tablespoons ground aniseed
2 teaspoons ground ginger
½ teaspoon ground cinnamon
½ teaspoon ground black cardamon seeds
4 green cardamoms

For best results use meat from a leg of lamb. Cut it into 3·5-cm/1½-in cubes then
rinse the meat and dry it thoroughly on absorbent kitchen paper. Heat the
mustard oil in a heavy-based saucepan. Add the cloves and asafoetida, cook for
a few seconds, then add the meat. Stand well back as the meat may splutter.
Stirring continuously, fry the meat until lightly browned.

Lightly whisk the yogurt and stir it carefully into the meat. Stirring
frequently, cook for 10–15 minutes until the oil begins to separate out. Add
the chilli powder, salt, ground aniseed and the ground ginger. Mix all the
ingredients together thoroughly, reduce the heat and cover with a tight-fitting
lid. Cook gently for 30–40 minutes until the meat is tender.

Sprinkle the ground cinnamon and black cardamom seeds over and stir-fry
for a few minutes, then cover and cook for 1–2 minutes to infuse the hot
spices. Remove the seeds from the green cardamom pods and lightly crush
them, discarding the pods. Sprinkle the crushed seeds over the dish before
serving.

Baingan Bhartha
Roasted aubergines

This recipe is a classic one from north India. The aubergines (eggplants) are first roasted over a naked flame, peeled and chopped, then mixed with onions, tomatoes, herbs and spices. The flavour of these roasted aubergines is quite delicious when they are cooked just to perfection.
Serve with Parathas (page 122).

SERVES 4 · PREPARATION TIME 15 MINUTES · COOKING TIME 45 MINUTES

2 large round aubergines (eggplants)
225 g/8 oz ($\frac{1}{2}$ lb) onions
small piece fresh root ginger
225 g/8 oz ($\frac{1}{2}$ lb) tomatoes or 1 (227-g/
  8-oz) can tomatoes, drained
2−3 tablespoons oil

1 teaspoon cumin seeds
1 green chilli (chili pepper) − optional
salt to taste
$\frac{1}{2}$ teaspoon chilli powder
1 tablespoon chopped fresh coriander
  leaves

Place the aubergines on metal skewers or on the end of a fondue fork and, using an oven glove, hold them over a low gas flame. Cook, turning the aubergines frequently and taking care not to burn your hand, until the skin is charred on all sides. The flavour of the vegetables is improved considerably if they are roasted over charcoal. Alternatively, the aubergines may be cooked under a very hot grill (broiler). Cool the aubergines slightly then carefully peel off the blistered skin. Discard the stalk and roughly chop the flesh.

Finely chop the onions, ginger and tomatoes. Heat the oil in a heavy-based frying pan (skillet), add the cumin seeds and cook them quickly until they pop. Stir in the onions, ginger and green chilli, if used. Stirring frequently, gently fry the onions to a rich golden colour without over-browning them. Add the aubergine, stir-fry the mixture for a few minutes then season it generously with salt and the chilli powder. Finally, stir in the tomatoes and make sure that all the ingredients are thoroughly mixed together. Reduce the heat and cover the pan, then allow the bhartha to cook gently for 15−20 minutes. Stir the mixture occasionally to prevent it from sticking to the pan − it is cooked when the oil separates out. Lightly stir the Baingan Bhartha and transfer it to a warmed serving dish then serve it immediately, sprinkled with freshly chopped coriander leaves.

Phool Gobi Aaloo

Spiced cauliflower and potatoes

(Illustrated on the front cover)
Fresh or frozen cauliflower is available all the year round. This dry vegetable curry combines small florets of cauliflower with potatoes and tomatoes. It is easy to prepare and tastes simply delicious – particularly when it is made with small new potatoes.
Serve with Murghi Bade Sabha (page 13), Chapatis (page 122) and Dall (page 121).

SERVES 4 · PREPARATION TIME 10 MINUTES · COOKING TIME 30 MINUTES

1 medium cauliflower
2 medium potatoes or 675 g/1½ lb small new potatoes
small piece fresh root ginger
2 ripe tomatoes
2 tablespoons oil
½ teaspoon cumin seeds

¼ teaspoon nigella seeds
¼ teaspoon mustard seeds
½ teaspoon turmeric
salt to taste
chilli powder to taste
1 tablespoon chopped coriander leaves

Trim the stalks from the cauliflower and break it into small florets. The stalks may be reserved to make Dandal (page 115). Peel or scrape the potatoes, cut old ones into 2·5-cm/1-in cubes or leave new potatoes whole. Finely chop the ginger and roughly chop the tomatoes.

Heat the oil in a heavy-based saucepan, add the cumin, nigella and the mustard seeds and cook them quickly until they pop – it should only take a few seconds. Add the ginger. Stir-fry for a few seconds before adding the turmeric, then season the spices to taste with salt and chilli powder. Cook for a minute before adding the tomatoes and continue to cook for about another minute until they are slightly softened. Add the cauliflower and potatoes to the pan, mix well to coat the vegetables with the spices, then reduce the heat. Cover the saucepan and leave the vegetables to cook for 15 minutes or until they are soft and any excess moisture is absorbed. Spoon the spiced vegetables carefully into a warmed serving dish, sprinkle the chopped coriander leaves over the top and serve the dish immediately with the suggested main dishes or any other meat or poultry curries.

Mattar Paneer
Cheese and peas in spicy sauce

Although commercially produced cheese is beginning to gain popularity in India, home-made cheese – similar to the cottage cheese and soft curd cheese of the West – has always been a favourite and forms the basis of a whole variety of Indian sweetmeats and desserts. It is also a vital ingredient in this classic savoury recipe.

SERVES 4 · PREPARATION TIME 2 DAYS · COOKING TIME 45 MINUTES

225 g/8 oz (1 cup) Paneer (page 118)
oil for deep frying
2 medium onions
small piece fresh root ginger
1 clove garlic
100g/4 oz (¼ lb) fresh tomatoes or
  1 (227-g/8-oz) can tomatoes
3 tablespoons oil
1 teaspoon cumin seeds

½ teaspoon chilli powder
1½ teaspoons ground coriander
½ teaspoon turmeric
salt to taste
1 tablespoon chopped coriander leaves
225 g/8 oz (1½ cups) lightly cooked fresh
  (or frozen) peas
600 ml/1 pint (2½ cups) water

Make the paneer according to the recipe instructions, allowing it to drain overnight. Line a sieve with scalded muslin (cheesecloth) and place the cheese in it. Fold over the muslin to cover the cheese completely and weight it down to remove any excess moisture from the cheese. Leave it to drain for 2–3 hours and chill until firm. Cut the cheese into neat 2·5-cm/1-in cubes.

Heat the oil to 180 c/350 f and carefully add the cheese cubes. Fry for 1–2 minutes until golden brown and crisp, then drain them and set aside. Mince the onions with the ginger and garlic. Finely chop the tomatoes, draining them first if using canned ones. Heat the oil in a heavy-based saucepan, add the cumin seeds and cook gently until they pop. Add the minced onion mixture and, stirring frequently, fry gently until it turns a rich golden colour. Take care not to over-brown the onion. Add the chilli powder, ground coriander, turmeric and salt to the pan. Stir-fry for a few seconds, then add the tomatoes and half the chopped coriander leaves. Stirring continuously, fry this mixture until the tomatoes are reduced to a pulp, adding a little water if necessary. The sauce is ready when the oil starts to separate out.

Add the peas, lower the heat and cover the pan. Steam-cook them for a few minutes before adding the water. Give the mixture a good stir, bring it to the boil, then lower the heat again and add the fried cheese cubes. Cover the pan and let the curry simmer gently for at least 20 minutes, until the sauce has thickened and the paneer has absorbed some of the sauce. Serve hot, sprinkled with the remaining coriander leaves.

West India

Dhan Sakh

Spiced chicken with legumes and vegetables

This classic Parsee recipe shows the happy blend of two cultures. Parsees, who are non-vegetarian, have adopted the Gujarati vegetarian spices and ingredients and combine them in this dish that has become popular all over the world for the subtlety of its flavour. This recipe also works well with lamb.
Serve with plain boiled rice.

SERVES 4 · PREPARATION TIME 1 HOUR · COOKING TIME 1¼ HOURS

100 g/4 oz (½ cup) toovar dall
25g/1 oz (2 tablespoons) each chana,
    moong and masoor dall
450 g/1 lb chicken meat
175 g/6 oz (½ lb) mixed vegetables,
    for example aubergine (eggplant),
    pumpkin, marrow (summer squash),
    fresh or frozen spinach
salt to taste
750 ml/1½ pints (3¾ cups) water

1 medium onion
2 tablespoons ghee (page 118)
1 tablespoon ground coriander
1 teaspoon ground cumin
½ teaspoon turmeric
½ teaspoon chilli powder
½ teaspoon ground ginger
pinch of garlic powder
3 tablespoons tamarind juice (page 119)

Thoroughly rinse and drain all the dall then cover with water and leave to soak for 30 minutes. Trim any fat off the chicken meat and cut it into small pieces. Prepare the vegetables. Remove the stalk from the aubergine and peel the pumpkin or marrow then cut into cubes similar in size to the meat. Drain the dalls, place them in a pan with the meat or poultry, vegetables, salt and water. Bring to the boil, reduce the heat and cover the pan with a tight-fitting lid. Simmer gently for 40–50 minutes or until the meat is tender and dalls have blended. Remove from the heat and carefully lift out all the meat. Reduce the dall mixture to a smooth purée in a liquidiser. Return the purée and meat to the pan and allow to simmer gently while preparing the spice mixture.

Slice the onion finely. Heat the ghee, add the onion and stir-fry to a rich golden brown. Add all the spices and cook gently for a few minutes, stirring frequently to prevent the mixture from sticking to the pan. Carefully pour the dall and meat mixture over and stir to mix well. Cover, and cook the Dhan Sakh gently for 5 minutes until thoroughly heated. Add the tamarind juice, stir thoroughly and heat for 1–2 minutes.

Pork Vindaloo

Pork in hot chilli sauce

Goa, a Portuguese territory until 1956, has a very special cuisine of its own. It is a mixture of both Portuguese and Indian cooking. Since the population is mainly Christian, pork is accepted and widely used. Vindaloo is world famous for its fiery heat and should be served with plain boiled rice.

SERVES 4 · PREPARATION TIME 30 MINUTES · COOKING TIME 1–1¼ HOURS

2 red chillies (chili peppers)
1 teaspoon cumin seeds
1 teaspoon coriander seeds
2 cloves
4 black peppercorns
2·5-cm/1-in stick cinnamon
2 cloves garlic

2·5-cm/1-in piece fresh root ginger
3 tablespoons vinegar
2 medium onions
450 g/1 lb lean pork
750 ml/1½ pints (3¾ cups) water
3 tablespoons oil
salt to taste

Remove the stalks from the chillies and place them in a heavy-based frying pan together with the cumin and coriander seeds, cloves, peppercorns and cinnamon stick. Cook over very gentle heat, stirring frequently, until well roasted, then grind these spices to a powder along with the garlic, ginger and vinegar.

Finely chop the onions. Trim any excess fat off the pork and cut it into 5-cm/ 2-in cubes. Place the meat in a pan with the water and bring it to the boil. Reduce the heat, cover and simmer gently for 45–50 minutes until the meat is tender, then strain it, reserving the cooking liquid.

In another pan, heat the oil, add the onions, season generously and stir-fry until golden brown. Add the ground ingredients and cook for a further 2–3 minutes, then stir in the boiled pork and mix well. Cover and cook gently for a further 15 minutes until the pork is very tender and has absorbed the flavour from the sauce. If more sauce is required some of the reserved cooking liquid may be added with the pork.

Aaloo Tarivale
Simple potato curry

This simple yet delicious potato dish is made by first boiling the potatoes in their skins. They are then peeled, cut into cubes and simmered in a thin sauce made of fresh or canned tomatoes, coriander and other herbs and spices. Unlike most curries, onions, ginger and garlic are not used to thicken this dish.
These potatoes are traditionally served with Pooris (page 116) and freshly made Mango Chutney (page 21).

SERVES 4 · PREPARATION TIME 5–10 MINUTES · COOKING TIME 50 MINUTES

450 g/1 lb potatoes	salt to taste
2 tablespoons oil	chilli powder to taste
1 teaspoon cumin seeds	$\frac{1}{2}$ teaspoon turmeric
$\frac{1}{4}$ teaspoon nigella seeds	225 g/8 oz ($\frac{1}{2}$ lb) tomatoes or
$\frac{1}{2}$ teaspoon mustard seeds	1 (227-g/8-oz) can tomatoes
1$\frac{1}{2}$ teaspoons ground coriander	900 ml/1$\frac{1}{2}$ pints (3$\frac{3}{4}$ cups) water

Scrub the potatoes and boil them in their skins for about 15 minutes. Cool them, then peel and cut them into small cubes.

Heat the oil, add the cumin, nigella and mustard seeds. As soon as the seeds pop, add the ground coriander, salt, chilli powder and turmeric. Roughly chop the tomatoes, chopping the canned tomatoes with their juice. Stir the spice mixture and add the tomatoes. Stir-fry for a few seconds then add 300 ml/ $\frac{1}{2}$ pint (1$\frac{1}{4}$ cups) of the water. Stir thoroughly and bring it to the boil. If fresh tomatoes are used they should be cooked until reduced to a pulp. Add the remaining water and bring it back to the boil. Reduce the heat, stir in the potatoes and allow the curry to simmer for 20–30 minutes or until the sauce has thickened slightly and the potatoes have absorbed the flavour. Serve immediately.

Bhindi Pyaz
Okra with onions

(Illustrated on page 41)
Many good supermarkets and greengrocers sell okra or ladyfingers and although they can be bought in cans, they taste best fresh. If the tapered ends of fresh okra snap off readily then they are young and tender, but if they do not the outer green skin may be fibrous and tough.
Serve with Chapatis (page 122) and Chana Dall (page 45).

SERVES 4 · PREPARATION TIME 10 MINUTES · COOKING TIME 20–30 MINUTES

450 g/1 lb okra or ladyfingers	$\frac{1}{2}$ teaspoon turmeric
3 medium onions	$\frac{1}{2}$ teaspoon chilli powder
3 tablespoons oil	salt to taste
1 teaspoon cumin seeds	2 tomatoes, roughly chopped

Thoroughly wash the okra and carefully dry them on absorbent kitchen paper. Cut off and discard the stalk end, then cut them into 5-mm/$\frac{1}{4}$-in thick slices. Thickly slice the onions.

Heat the oil in a heavy-based frying pan (skillet). Add the cumin seeds and cook for a few seconds until they pop. Add the onions and stir-fry until they are a pale golden brown. Add the okra, turmeric, chilli powder, salt and tomatoes and stir-fry for a few minutes until all the ingredients are well mixed. Cover, reduce the heat to its lowest setting and cook for about 10 minutes. Okra cooks very quickly – do not overcook it or it will break up. Serve hot.

Mango Chutney

Chutneys and pickles form a very important part of any Indian meal and this simple yet delicious chutney is a basic accompaniment for most curries.

SERVES 4 · PREPARATION TIME 10 MINUTES

2 green mangoes	small bunch coriander leaves
1 medium onion	salt to taste
1 green chilli (chili pepper)	

Peel the mangoes and cut them into small pieces, discarding the stone. Peel and chop the onion, and chop the green chilli. Wash and coarsely chop the coriander leaves. Place all the ingredients together in a liquidiser, adding 2 tablespoons water, and blend the mixture to a smooth paste.

Central India

Pasinde Sade

Simple lamb in spices

(Illustrated on page 41)
Lean, tender meat from a leg of lamb should be used for this truly delicious dish which is rich in its use of ghee, onions and coriander. The cooked recipe may be cooled and frozen for up to 3 months.
Serve with plain boiled rice or Chapatis (page 122) and Imli aur Podina Chutney (page 26).

SERVES 4 · PREPARATION TIME 2¼ HOURS · COOKING TIME 1¼ HOURS

450 g/1 lb lean lamb off the leg
2 tablespoons natural yogurt
3 medium onions
3 tablespoons ghee (page 118)
1 teaspoon chilli powder
1½ teaspoons ground coriander

½ teaspoon garam masala (page 119)
salt to taste
bay leaf
1 litre/1¾ pints (4½ cups) water
2−3 tomatoes

Trim any excess fat off the meat and cut it into small cubes, then rinse and dry it thoroughly on absorbent kitchen paper. Lightly whisk the yogurt and pour it over the meat in a basin or small dish. Stir well to coat the meat thoroughly in the yogurt, then cover and leave it to marinate for 2 hours. Remove the meat from the yogurt marinade and reserve both.

Roughly chop the onions and grind them to a fine paste. Heat the ghee in a heavy-based saucepan, add the onion paste and cook to a golden brown. Add the chilli powder, coriander and garam masala then season it to taste with salt and stir in the bay leaf. Cook this mixture, stirring continuously, for a few minutes. Lightly beat the yogurt marinade and add it to the onion mixture. Continue cooking, stirring frequently, until most excess moisture has evaporated and the ghee begins to separate out. Add the meat and cook it in the fairly dry paste, stirring frequently, until it is well browned. Add the water and bring to the boil, then reduce the heat and cover the pan closely. Simmer the Pasinde Sade for 40−45 minutes until the sauce has thickened.

Peel and roughly chop the tomatoes, then add them to the lamb mixture. Stir well, reduce the heat then re-cover the pan and cook the meat for a further 10 minutes until it is tender. Remove the lamb to a warmed serving dish and serve it immediately with the suggested accompaniments.

Shidumpukth Gosht (Do Piaza)
Meat in rich onion sauce

This superb dish is appropriately named, since Do Piaza means 'meat cooked with double the quantity of onions'. It is an extremely rich and delicious dish and one that will grace any table.
Serve with Parathas (page 122).

SERVES 4 · PREPARATION TIME 15 MINUTES · COOKING TIME 2 HOURS

1·25 kg/2½ lb onions
450 g/1 lb tender boneless meat,
    for example lamb, steak or pork
4 tablespoons oil
salt to taste
2 tablespoons ground coriander
1 tablespoon chilli powder

1 clove garlic, crushed
2 bay leaves
salt to taste
2 tablespoons freshly squeezed lemon
    juice
2 tablespoons chopped coriander leaves

Finely chop 900 g/2 lb of the onions. Cut the meat into 3·5-cm/1½-in cubes and rinse it, then drain and dry it on absorbent kitchen paper. Grease a heavy-based saucepan with a little of the oil. Layer the onions and meat alternately in the saucepan, reserving enough onion for the top layer. Sprinkle the salt, ground coriander and chilli powder on top of the final layer of meat before topping with the reserved onions. Cover with a tight-fitting lid and cook over very gentle heat for 1½–2 hours until the onions are reduced to a pulp and the meat is tender. There is no need to add any water to this dish as the onions produce enough moisture. Remove the meat from the sauce and reserve both.

Finely chop the remaining onions. Heat the remaining oil, add the onions, garlic, bay leaves and salt. Stir-fry until the onions turn a rich golden brown in colour, then add the cooked meat and cook, stirring frequently, until the meat browns. Pour in the reserved sauce and lemon juice, and stir-fry for a further two minutes. Sprinkle with freshly chopped coriander leaves before serving.

Dall Pakori Ki Sabji
Dall fritters in spicy sauce

*Pulses can be used in all sorts of interesting dishes. They can be ground and
made into dumplings for frying, then cooked in a spicy sauce as in this dish.
Alternatively, they can be cooked with a variety of vegetables, meat, poultry and
fish. They are especially valuable to the vegetarian diet as most pulses are very
rich in protein.*
Serve with Chapatis (page 122).

SERVES 4 · PREPARATION TIME 1 DAY · COOKING TIME 1 HOUR

225 g/8 oz (1 cup) split moong dall, in
   their skins
oil for deep frying
3 medium onions
small piece fresh root ginger
3 tablespoons oil
1 teaspoon cumin seeds

½ teaspoon chilli powder
½ teaspoon turmeric
1 teaspoon ground coriander
salt to taste
3 tablespoons natural yogurt
750 ml/1¼ pints (3 cups) water
1 tablespoon chopped coriander leaves

Wash the dall thoroughly and leave them to soak overnight in plenty of cold
water. Carefully remove the green skins that have loosened from the dall and
floated to the surface of the water. Discard these and wash the dall in several
changes of water in order to loosen any remaining skins. Drain thoroughly.
Grind the dall to a fine thick paste, adding a few drops of water if necessary.
Place the paste in a bowl and beat it thoroughly with either your hand or a
wooden spoon. This will lighten the mixture and make the fried dumplings
light and fluffy. Test the lightness of the mixture by dropping a small spoonful
of it into a bowl of water. If the mixture floats to the surface, it is light enough,
but if it sinks it needs more beating.

Heat the oil for deep frying to 180 c/350 f. Cook small spoonfuls of the
mixture in the oil, turning once or twice, until the dumplings are a rich golden
brown. Drain them carefully on absorbent kitchen paper and set them aside.

Finely chop the onions and the ginger. Heat the oil then add the cumin seeds
and cook quickly until they pop. Stir in the onions and ginger and stir-fry until
they turn a rich golden. Add the chilli powder, turmeric, ground coriander
and salt and stir-fry for a few seconds. Lightly beat the yogurt and add to the
pan, then cook, stirring frequently, until the yogurt is well blended and the oil
starts to separate out. Add the water, bring it to the boil, then reduce the heat
and let the mixture simmer gently for 10 minutes.

Add the fried dumplings and cook over a low heat for a further few minutes
until the dumplings absorb some of the sauce. Do not overcook the dumplings
or they may break up. Serve hot, sprinkled with finely chopped fresh
coriander leaves.

Jimi Kandh
Yam in yogurt and spices

In this dish the yams are cooked in a very rich sauce normally used for meat dishes and they are frequently mistaken for chunks of tender lamb. Serve with Tarka rice (page 26), Chapatis (page 122) or Naan (page 123).

SERVES 4 · PREPARATION TIME 30 MINUTES · COOKING TIME 1 HOUR

450 g/1 lb tender yam
1–2 tablespoons salt
oil for deep frying
2 medium onions
small piece fresh root ginger
1 clove garlic
2–3 tablespoons oil
1 teaspoon cumin seeds
3 cloves
2 green cardamoms
bay leaf
4 black peppercorns

2·5-cm/1-in stick cinnamon
1 teaspoon turmeric
½ teaspoon chilli powder
1 teaspoon ground coriander
½ teaspoon garam masala (page 119)
salt to taste
100 g/4 oz (¼ lb) tomatoes or
   1 (227-g/8-oz) can tomatoes
4 tablespoons natural yogurt
600 ml/1 pint (2½ cups) water
1 tablespoon chopped coriander leaves

Before peeling the thick skin off the yam, rub the palms of your hands with a little oil to prevent any irritation developing from touching the vegetable. Peel the yam and cut it into 2·5-cm/1-in cubes, then place in a colander and sprinkle it liberally with the salt. Allow to stand for 10–15 minutes in order to drain away any excess moisture, then dry thoroughly on absorbent kitchen paper.

Heat the oil for deep frying to 180 c/350 f and cook the yam cubes, a few at a time, until golden brown. Drain them on absorbent kitchen paper and set aside. Finely chop the onion, ginger and garlic. Heat the 2–3 tablespoons oil, add the cumin seeds and cook, stirring continuously, until they begin to splutter. Add the onion, ginger and garlic and cook over a gentle heat until the onion is a rich golden colour. Add all the spices and season with salt to taste. Continue to cook for a few seconds, then add the tomatoes, roughly chopped. Stirring frequently, cook the mixture for a few minutes until the tomatoes have softened. (If you are using fresh tomatoes, add 2 tablespoons water).

Lightly whisk the yogurt and add it to the mixture, stirring well. Continue to cook, stirring frequently, until the sauce turns a rich colour and the oil starts to separate out. Add the water, mix well and bring it to the boil. Allow it to boil for a few minutes, then add the fried yam cubes. Stir thoroughly, reduce the heat and cover the pan. Cook the Jimi Kandh gently for 20–30 minutes until the sauce has thickened and the yam has absorbed some of the sauce. Serve hot, sprinkled with freshly chopped coriander leaves.

Tarka Rice

This dish combines aromatic spices and perfectly cooked rice.

SERVES 4 · PREPARATION TIME 40–50 MINUTES · COOKING TIME 25–30 MINUTES

275 g/10 oz (1¼ cups) Basmati or Patna
  rice
1 medium onion
1 tablespoon ghee (page 118)
1 teaspoon cumin seeds
3–4 whole black peppercorns
3–4 cloves

2·5-cm/1-in stick cinnamon
bay leaf
2–3 whole green cardamoms
about 750 ml/1¼ pints (generous 3 cups)
  water
½ teaspoon salt

Rinse the rice thoroughly and soak it in fresh water for at least 30–40 minutes. Slice the onion thinly. Heat the ghee in a heavy-based saucepan, then add the onions and stir-fry until pale golden. Add all the spices and, stirring frequently, continue to fry until the onions are a rich golden colour and the spices have given off their aroma.

Drain the rice and add to the onion mixture. Stir-fry for a minute, then pour in enough water to come about 1 in/2·5 cm over the top of the rice. Add the salt. Bring to the boil then reduce the heat, cover closely and cook gently for 20–30 minutes until the rice is tender and all the water has been absorbed. Fluff up the rice with a fork and serve at once.

Imli aur Podina Chutney
Tamarind and mint chutney

(Illustrated on page 41)

SERVES 4 · PREPARATION TIME 40 MINUTES

50 g/2 oz (½ cup) tamarind
150 ml/¼ pint (⅔ cup) water
1½ teaspoons sugar

1½ teaspoons salt
1 teaspoon chilli powder
2 teaspoons dried mint

Soak the tamarind in warm water for 30 minutes. Use your fingers to squeeze all the pulp out of the tamarind, then strain it through a fine sieve and reserve the liquid. Discard all the stones and fibres.

Mix all the remaining ingredients together with the reserved liquid and chill slightly before serving. This chutney may be stored in an airtight container in the refrigerator for up to 2 weeks.

East India

Malai Chinghri
Prawns in coconut milk

*The Bay of Bengal boasts the finest king prawns to be found anywhere.
When cooked in creamy coconut milk, these prawns just melt in the mouth.
Serve with plain boiled rice.*

SERVES 4 · PREPARATION TIME 20 MINUTES · COOKING TIME 40–50 MINUTES

450 g/1 lb peeled king prawns
1½ teaspoons salt
1½ teaspoons tumeric
small piece fresh root ginger
1 medium onion, peeled and quartered

1 green chilli (chili pepper)
2 tablespoons mustard oil
1 tablespoon ghee (page 118)
2 medium potatoes
150 ml/¼ pint (⅔ cup) thick coconut milk

Rinse and dry the prawns on absorbent kitchen paper. Mix together one teaspoon each of salt and turmeric and rub this into the prawns.

Grind the ginger, onion, green chilli and remaining turmeric into a smooth paste. Heat the oil in a heavy-based frying pan (skillet) or saucepan, add the prawns and fry, turning frequently until they are a golden colour. Drain them on absorbent kitchen paper and set aside. Discard the oil, wipe the pan then add the ghee. When it is hot add the paste and cook it, stirring frequently, until it turns golden in colour.

Meanwhile peel and quarter the potatoes. Add the fried prawns to the paste together with the potatoes and stir-fry them for a few seconds before seasoning with the remaining salt. Stir in the coconut milk, cover the pan closely and reduce the heat. Cook the dish gently for 20–30 minutes or until the potatoes are tender. Transfer the curry to a warmed serving dish and serve it immediately.

Note: Small peeled prawns or shrimps can be substituted for the expensive king prawns and the cooked dish may be frozen for 2–3 months. If it is to be frozen, omit the potatoes and cook them in the defrosted curry.

Kabli Chane
Whole spiced chick peas

(Illustrated on page 41)
Chick peas are a favourite in India and are either curried or cooked in dry masala, or eaten as a spicy fried snack.
Serve with plain boiled rice and natural yogurt.

SERVES 4 · PREPARATION 1 DAY · COOKING TIME 1½ HOURS

225 g/8 oz (1 cup) chick peas
1 litre/2 pints (5 cups) water
1 teaspoon salt
2 large onions
small piece fresh root ginger
1 clove garlic
1 green chilli (chili pepper) – optional
225 g/8 oz (½ lb) tomatoes or 1 (227-g/8-oz) can tomatoes
3 tablespoons oil

1 teaspoon cumin seeds
½ teaspoon mustard seeds
¼ teaspoon nigella seeds
1½ teaspoons ground coriander
½ teaspoon tumeric
½ teaspoon chilli powder
salt to taste
1 tablespoon chopped coriander leaves
1 teaspoon garam masala (page 119)

Soak the chick peas in plenty of cold water overnight or for up to 24 hours. The longer the chick peas are soaked the quicker they will cook. Drain and thoroughly rinse them discarding any that have not swollen, then place them in a large saucepan with the water and salt. Bring to the boil and simmer for 50 minutes, or until the peas are tender.

While the peas are cooking, finely chop the onions, ginger, garlic, green chilli (if used) and tomatoes. Heat the oil, add the cumin, mustard and nigella seeds and cook, stirring frequently until they pop. Add the finely chopped onion, ginger and garlic. Stirring frequently, fry this mixture until the onion turns golden brown. Care must be taken not to overbrown this mixture or the garlic will turn bitter.

Add the remaining spices and salt, but not the garam masala. Stir-fry for a minute then add the chopped tomatoes. Stirring frequently, cook this mixture until the tomatoes are reduced to a pulp – it is cooked as soon as the oil separates out. Pour it into the pan containing the chick peas and their cooking liquid, then stir well to mix all the ingredients thoroughly. Return the pan to the heat, cover and simmer gently for 10 minutes until the sauce thickens and the chick peas have absorbed some of the flavour. Serve immediately sprinkled with chopped coriander leaves and garam masala.

Shag Bhaja
Lightly fried spinach

Tender spinach leaves are a delight to eat and taste especially good without the addition of strong spices.
Serve with Dall (page 121) and Pooris (page 116).

SERVES 4 · PREPARATION TIME 10 MINUTES · COOKING TIME 10 MINUTES

450 g/1 lb small, tender spinach leaves
2 tablespoons oil
1 teaspoon panch foran (see below)

1 green chilli (1 chili pepper)
pinch of sugar
1 teaspoon salt

Thoroughly wash and drain the spinach leaves. Heat the oil, add the panch foran and cook gently, stirring frequently until the seeds pop. Cut the green chilli in half, remove and discard the stalk and seeds, then add it to the pan together with the sugar and salt. Stir-fry over low heat for 5 minutes until the spinach is cooked.

Panch Foran

This combination of five spices is commonly used in Bengali dishes from eastern India. The spices can be left whole or ground to a fine powder.

MAKES 275 G/10 OZ · PREPARATION TIME 5–10 MINUTES

50 g/2 oz (6 tablespoons) aniseeds
50 g/2 oz (6 tablespoons) nigella seeds
50 g/2 oz (6 tablespoons) fenugreek seeds

50 g/2 oz (6 tablespoons) mustard seeds
50 g/2 oz (6 tablespoons) cumin seeds

Mix all the spices together and store them in an airtight jar for up to a month. Use as required.

South India

Talawa Gosht
Fried beef or lamb

Hyderabad in the south of India boasts a fine tradition of meat cookery.
This particular dish is simple and easy to make and absolutely delicious.
Serve with Sem Rai (see page 32).

SERVES 4 · PREPARATION TIME 10 MINUTES · COOKING TIME 1–1¼ HOURS

450 g/1 lb braising steak (chuck steak or
    blade beef) or boneless lamb
small piece fresh root ginger
2 cloves garlic, crushed
½ teaspoon turmeric

salt to taste
1 litre/1¾ pints (4½ cups) water
4 tablespoons oil
chilli powder to taste
1 tablespoon chopped coriander leaves

Rinse the meat and cut it into 2·5-cm/1-in cubes, then place it in a saucepan with the ginger (in one piece), garlic, turmeric, salt and water.

Bring the water to the boil, reduce the heat and simmer the Talawa Gosht uncovered for 40–50 minutes until the meat is tender and the liquid well reduced. Strain the meat, reserving the stock for future use and discard the ginger.

Heat the oil, add the meat and, stirring continuously, fry until browned on all sides. Add the chilli powder and stir-fry for a few minutes. Serve hot, sprinkled with fresh coriander leaves.

Dum Ke Ande
Whole eggs in spices

*I have found very few successful spiced dishes using eggs. This recipe is
exceptionally successful and the spicy sauce enhances both the flavour of the eggs
and the look of the dish.*
Serve with Zaffron Pullao (page 120) or Dall (page 121).

SERVES 4 · PREPARATION TIME 10 MINUTES · COOKING TIME 40 MINUTES

1 medium onion
65 g/2½ oz (5 tablespoons) ghee (page 118)
½ teaspoon ground ginger
1 clove garlic, crushed
40 g/1½ oz (⅓ cup) blanched almonds
1 tablespoon poppy seeds
½ teaspoon turmeric

salt to taste
chilli powder to taste
100 ml/4 fl oz (½ cup) natural yogurt,
   lightly whisked
4 eggs
1 tablespoon freshly chopped coriander
   leaves

Roughly chop the onion. Heat the ghee in a large heavy-based frying pan
(skillet), add the onion, ginger, garlic, almonds and poppy-seeds. Stir-fry until
the onions turn a rich golden colour, then use a slotted spoon to remove the
mixture from the pan reserving the ghee. Grind the cooked onion mixture to a
smooth paste then return it to the ghee in the pan and stir-fry for a few
minutes. Stir in the turmeric and season to taste with salt and chilli powder,
then allow to cook for a minute before adding the yogurt. Stirring
continuously, fry this mixture until all the yogurt is absorbed and the ghee
starts to separate out.

Lightly smooth the surface of the mixture and carefully break the eggs on
top. Reduce the heat to its lowest setting, cover the pan and cook for 25
minutes or until the eggs are set. Sprinkle the cooked eggs with the freshly
chopped coriander leaves and serve immediately.

The eggs may also be cooked in the oven. Transfer the cooked onion mixture
to a lightly greased, shallow, ovenproof dish and spread it evenly over the
base. Break the eggs on top and cover the dish. Bake in a moderate oven (180 C,
350 F, Gas 4) for 20–25 minutes.

Sem Rai

Runner beans with mustard seeds

*Both mustard seeds and powder are used in large quantities in Indian cooking.
Serve this dish with plain boiled rice.*

SERVES 4 · PREPARATION TIME 15 MINUTES · COOKING TIME 20 MINUTES

25 g/1 oz plus $\frac{1}{2}$ teaspoon mustard
  seeds
1 clove garlic
1 green chilli (chili pepper)

450 g/1 lb tender runner beans
salt to taste
2 tablespoons mustard oil
chilli powder to taste

Grind the 25 g/1 oz mustard seeds, garlic and green chilli to a fine paste. Top,
tail and string the runner beans, then cut them into 5-cm/2-in lengths. Place
them in a saucepan with the salt and add just enough water to cover the beans.
Bring it to the boil, cover the pan and reduce the heat, then simmer for 5–10
minutes until the beans are tender.

    Heat the mustard oil, add the remaining $\frac{1}{2}$ teaspoon mustard seeds and cook
quickly until they pop. Add the chilli powder, shake the pan for a second then
add the tender runner beans and all their cooking liquid. Finally add the mustard
seed paste and mix well. Cover and cook for 2–3 minutes then serve hot.

Sambar Powder

Buy or make sambar powder in small quantities.

MAKES 175–225 G/6–8 OZ · PREPARATION TIME 20 MINUTES

1 tablespoon chana dall
1 tablespoon urad dall
1 tablespoon toovar dall
2 tablespoons coriander seeds

1 tablespoon cumin seeds
1 tablespoon turmeric
50 g/2 oz ($\frac{1}{2}$ cup) chilli powder

Dry roast the dalls together with the coriander and cumin seeds in a heavy-
based frying pan (skillet) until pale golden in colour. Grind all the ingredients
to a fine powder and store in an airtight jar for up to a month.

Tomato Sambar

A sambar is a combination of pulses, vegetables, yogurt, tomatoes and spices.
Ready-mixed sambar powder may be purchased in oriental stores.
However, I give a basic recipe so you can make your own.

SERVES 4 · PREPARATION TIME 20 MINUTES · COOKING TIME 30–35 MINUTES

50 g/2 oz ($\frac{1}{4}$ cup) toovar dall	salt to taste
450 ml/$\frac{3}{4}$ pint (scant 2 cups) water	chilli powder to taste
450 g/1 lb tomatoes	4 curry leaves
1 tablespoon tamarind juice	1 tablespoon oil
1$\frac{1}{2}$ tablespoons sambar powder (page 32)	1 teaspoon urad dall
$\frac{1}{2}$ teaspoon turmeric	1 teaspoon fenugreek seeds
small pinch asafoetida	1 teaspoon mustard seeds

Thoroughly rinse and drain the toovar dall, then soak them for 15 minutes and drain carefully. Transfer them to a saucepan, add the water and bring it to the boil, then simmer the dall for 15–20 minutes or until they are almost tender. Quarter the tomatoes and add them to the dall, then cook until they are reduced to a pulp. Add the remaining ingredients except the oil, urad dall, fenugreek and mustard seed. Stir well and cook for a few minutes, then reduce the heat and simmer gently for a further 10 minutes.

Meanwhile, heat the oil, add the urad dall, fenugreek seeds and mustard seeds. Cook quickly, stirring frequently until the seeds pop. Top the simmering sambar with this garnish. Stir and serve immediately with plain boiled rice.

Anardana Chutney

Pomegranate chutney

SERVES 4 · PREPARATION TIME 15 MINUTES

50 g/2 oz (6 tablespoons) pomegranate seeds	$\frac{1}{2}$ teaspoon garam masala (page 119)
1 small onion	1 teaspoon chopped coriander leaves
$\frac{1}{2}$ teaspoon chilli powder	2–3 tablespoons water
	salt to taste

Rinse and drain the seeds, taking care not to rub off their outer coating. Peel and roughly chop the onion then put it in a liquidiser together with the pomegranate seeds and all the remaining ingredients. Blend the mixture to a purée – the chutney will retain a certain amount of texture as the seeds do not become absolutely smooth. Serve freshly made.

Pakistan

It is not surprising that the curries of Pakistan have much in common with those of India, since until the end of British rule and the partition of India in 1947 they were one country, sharing a similar culture.

The religion of Pakistan is predominantly Muslim and though pork is not eaten, lamb, beef and poultry are commonly used. As most of the people are non-vegetarian, the art of cooking rich meat and poultry dishes is similar to that practised by the Muslims in India. Plenty of ghee (clarified butter) is used in their kormas, biriyanis and pullaos, together with various spices and herbs. There is very little vegetarian cooking and where vegetables are included they are either highly spiced or mixed with minced meat or poultry.

Pakistani cooking is an intricate art. The ingredients are painstakingly selected, mixed, blended and marinated; rich sauces are based on the extravagant use of onions combined with ginger, garlic, yogurt and tomatoes – similar ingredients to those used in India, but the different methods and cooking techniques give the dishes a totally unique and interesting character.

Among the recipes I have selected here are some of my own favourites, gathered during two happy years I spent in that country in my teens when, having become aware of good food and thoroughly enjoying it, I had a delightful time sampling my first rich Muslim cuisine.

Murghi Korma
Chicken korma

This is one of the best ways to cook chicken, as the flavour of the rich sauce enhances the delicate taste of the poultry.
Serve with plain boiled rice or Dall (page 121).

SERVES 4 · PREPARATION TIME 25 MINUTES · COOKING TIME 1½ HOURS

1 teaspoon poppy seeds
1 (1-kg/2¼–2½-lb) chicken
4 medium onions
3 cloves garlic
2·5-cm/1-in piece fresh root ginger
2 tablespoons desiccated coconut
2 green chillies (chili peppers)
½ teaspoon turmeric
50 g/2 oz (1 cup) fresh coriander
    leaves

3 tablespoons ghee (page 118)
3–4 cloves
2·5-cm/1-in stick cinnamon
2 black cardamoms
small pinch ground nutmeg
salt to taste
4 tablespoons natural yogurt, lightly
    whisked
450 ml/¾ pint (scant 2 cups) water
1 tablespoon lemon juice

Soak the poppy seeds in a little hot water for 15 minutes, then drain them thoroughly. Cut the unboned chicken into eight pieces. Thinly slice two of the onions. Grind the remaining onions with the garlic, ginger, coconut, poppy seeds, green chillies, turmeric and half the coriander leaves until they form a smooth paste. Coarsely chop the remaining coriander leaves.

Heat the ghee in a heavy-based saucepan. Add the cloves, cinnamon, cardamoms, nutmeg and salt. Stir-fry the spices for 2–3 minutes, then add the sliced onion. Continue to stir-fry until the onion is golden brown, then add the paste and continue to cook for a few more minutes. Add the chicken pieces, the chopped coriander leaves and yogurt and stir-fry for a few minutes until all the ingredients are well blended.

Pour in the measured water. Bring it to the boil, then reduce the heat and allow the korma to simmer, stirring occasionally, until the chicken is cooked and the sauce has thickened – about an hour. Stir in the lemon juice and serve immediately.

Mughlai Murgh
Mughlai chicken

*As a girl, I spent two years in Karachi – a gourmet's paradise. I had heard
about the rich traditional cooking of the Muslims, but I was unprepared for the
treats that lay in store. Delights like Mughlai chicken awaited me whenever I
was invited to dine with close family friends. Cooked in saffron-flavoured milk
and yogurt, this chicken dish is really delicious.
Serve with Parathas (page 122).*

SERVES 4 · PREPARATION TIME 45 MINUTES · COOKING TIME 1¼ HOURS

1 (1-kg/2¼-lb) chicken
2·5-cm/1-in piece fresh root ginger
3 cloves garlic
1 teaspoon chilli powder
salt to taste
150 ml/¼ pint (⅔ cup) milk
1 tablespoon single cream (light cream)
½ teaspoon saffron strands

300 ml/½ pint (1¼ cups) natural yogurt
2 large onions
50 g/2 oz (½ cup) blanched almonds,
    roasted
25 g/1 oz (¼ cup) pumpkin seeds, roasted
4–5 tablespoons ghee (page 118)
600 ml/1 pint (2½ cups) water

Skin the chicken and cut it into eight pieces. Grind the ginger, garlic, chilli
powder and salt to a smooth paste. Spread this paste evenly over the chicken
pieces and set aside.

Mix the milk with the cream, add the saffron strands and leave to stand for
10 minutes. Meanwhile, lightly whisk the yogurt. Pour the saffron-flavoured
milk and yogurt over the chicken, turning it over to coat it thoroughly. Leave
the chicken to marinate for 30 minutes.

Finely chop the onions. Grind the almonds and pumpkin seeds together to
form a smooth paste. Heat the ghee in a heavy-based pan, add the onion and
stir-fry to a golden brown. Add the marinated chicken with all the marinade.
Cover the pan, reduce the heat and cook gently until all the excess moisture
has evaporated – about 30–45 minutes. Add the nut and pumpkin seed paste
and mix well, then cook for a further few minutes, stirring all the time.

Pour in the water, bring it to the boil, stir again then reduce the heat, cover
and simmer gently until the chicken is tender and the sauce has thickened –
about 30 minutes.

Masala Murgh
Spiced chicken

An easy yet delicious dish to prepare; the chicken is first boiled with spices, then fried with onions.
Serve with Chapatis (page 122) and natural yogurt.

SERVES 4 · PREPARATION TIME 20 MINUTES · COOKING TIME 2 HOURS

1 (1-kg/2¼-lb) chicken
2 large onions
2·5-cm/1-in piece fresh root ginger
2 cloves garlic
salt to taste
chilli powder to taste
½ teaspoon turmeric

1 teaspoon garam masala (page 119)
1 teaspoon ground coriander
1 teaspoon ground cumin
2 teaspoons lemon juice
450 ml/¾ pint (scant 2 cups) water
2 tablespoons ghee (page 118) or oil

Cut the chicken into 8 pieces or leave whole if preferred. Grind one onion, the ginger and garlic to a smooth paste. Place the chicken in a large pan along with the salt, chilli powder, turmeric, garam masala, coriander and cumin. Add the onion paste and lemon juice and pour in the water. Bring it to the boil, lower the heat then simmer, uncovered, over very low heat until the chicken is tender and all the moisture has been absorbed. Remove the chicken from the pan, and set it aside, then thinly slice the remaining onion.

Heat the ghee or oil, add the onion and cooked chicken and fry, turning the chicken frequently, until both chicken and onions are golden in colour. Serve immediately.

Badshahi Seekh Kebabs
Royal Seekh kebabs

(Illustrated on page 42)
I have eaten a variety of kebabs from many different countries but nothing quite matches these, appropriately named, for their outstanding flavour. Tender pieces of meat, marinated in herbs and spices, are served with a wonderful nutty creamy sauce.
Serve with Zaffran Pullao (page 120).

SERVES 4 · PREPARATION TIME 4½ HOURS · COOKING TIME 30 MINUTES

450 g/1 lb tender boneless lamb
1 medium onion
2·5-cm/1-in piece fresh root ginger
2 cloves garlic
½ teaspoon cumin seeds
small bunch coriander leaves
salt to taste

chilli powder to taste
10–12 shallots or very small onions
300 ml/½ pint (1¼ cups) full cream milk
25 g/1 oz (¼ cup) blanched almonds, chopped
4 tablespoons single cream (light cream)
2 green cardamoms

Trim any fat from the meat and cut it into 2·5-cm/1-in cubes. Grind the onion, ginger, garlic, cumin seeds, coriander leaves, salt and chilli powder together to give a fine paste. Mix the paste with the pieces of meat to coat them thoroughly, then leave them to marinate for 3–4 hours.

Thread the marinated meat cubes on to long metal skewers with the shallots or small onions in between. Cook under a medium-hot grill (broiler), turning frequently, or barbecue the kebabs over charcoal until the meat is well browned and tender.

Meanwhile, boil the milk with the chopped almonds in a heavy-based saucepan for a few minutes until it thickens slightly. Stir in the cream and heat gently for a few minutes, then transfer the sauce to a warmed sauceboat or bowl. Split the cardamoms and remove the seeds, crush them lightly and sprinkle them over the sauce. Arrange the kebabs on a serving dish and serve the sauce separately. Alternatively, remove the meat and onions from the skewers, arrange on a dish and serve with the sauce poured over.

Lamb Biriyani

A biriyani is a very rich and extremely satisfying rice dish which forms a complete meal by itself. Flavourings and essences like saffron and rosewater are essential ingredients in authentic biriyanis.

SERVES 4 · PREPARATION TIME 1 HOUR 40 MINUTES · COOKING TIME 1½ HOURS

450 g/1 lb (2 cups) basmati rice
450 g/1 lb lean boneless lamb
5 medium onions
1 teaspoon salt
1·15 litres/2 pints (5 cups) water
2·5-cm/1-in piece fresh root ginger
1 clove garlic
4 tablespoon ghee (page 118)
3 cloves

2·5-cm/1-in stick cinnamon
½ teaspoon black cumin seeds
1 black cardamom
2 green cardamoms
bay leaf
few strands of saffron
few drops of rosewater
1 small onion, thinly sliced

Wash the rice in several changes of water, then soak it in fresh water for about 1 hour. Cut the meat into 3·5-cm/1½-in cubes and chop three of the onions. Place both in a saucepan with the salt and water. Bring it to the boil and simmer gently until the meat is just tender – about 45 minutes. Drain the meat, reserving the stock, meat and onion pulp.

Grind the remaining onions, ginger and garlic together to a paste. Heat 2 tablespoons of the ghee in a large heavy-based saucepan, add the ground onion mixture, spices and bay leaf and stir-fry to a pale golden colour. Add the boiled meat and onion pulp. Stirring continuously, fry the mixture until the meat is a rich golden brown. Drain the rice and add it to the meat. Stir-fry for another few minutes until the rice browns, then pour in enough of the stock to come about 2·5 cm/1 in over the top of the rice and meat. Bring it to the boil, cover the pan with a tight-fitting lid and reduce the heat. Cook gently for 10 minutes or until the rice is half cooked. Dissolve the strands of saffron in a tablespoon of water and pour it over the rice. Gently mix the saffron into the rice with a fork – this will partly colour the rice. Add the rosewater, cover the pan and cook for a further 15–20 minutes.

Heat the remaining ghee, add the finely sliced onion and stir-fry until crisp and golden. Pour this over the rice just before serving.

Mutton Korma

Mutton and lamb are more widely eaten in Pakistan than beef. One of the traditional dishes that has earned world-wide popularity is Mutton Korma – delicious and requiring little effort to prepare and cook.
Serve with Chapatis (page 122) and Zaffran Pullao (page 120).

SERVES 4 · PREPARATION TIME 1½ HOURS · COOKING TIME 1½ HOURS

450 g/1 lb tender bonless lamb or mutton
350 g/12 oz (¾ lb) onions
2·5-cm/1-in piece fresh root ginger
2 cloves garlic, crushed
3–4 green cardamoms, lightly crushed
2 teaspoons coriander seeds
3–4 cloves

2·5-cm/1-in stick cinnamon
600 ml/1 pint (2½ cups) natural yogurt
salt to taste
chilli powder to taste
½ teaspoon turmeric
3 tablespoons ghee (page 118) or oil
bay leaf

Trim any fat and gristle from the meat and cut it into 2·5-cm/1-in pieces. Thinly slice the onions, mince or grate the ginger and mix both with the garlic, cardamoms, coriander seeds, cloves and cinnamon stick. Lightly whisk the yogurt and stir it into the onion mixture together with all the remaining ingredients except the ghee or oil and bay leaf. Pour this mixture over the meat, mix thoroughly and cover the dish, then leave it to marinate for at least an hour or up to 24 hours – the longer the better.

Heat the ghee or oil in a heavy-based saucepan. Lightly fry the bay leaf, then add the marinated meat together with the spiced yogurt marinade. Mix thoroughly and heat through, then reduce the heat and cover the pan with a tight-fitting lid. Cook the korma for 1–1½ hours, or until the meat is tender and all the excess moisture has been absorbed. At this stage the ghee will separate out to the top of the dish. Stir the ghee back into the sauce and serve immediately.

Clockwise from top right: Bhindi Pyaz (page 21), Kabli Chane (page 28), Imli aur Podina Chutney (page 26), Chapatis (page 122) and Pasinde Sade (page 22)

Keema Mattar
Spicy beef with green peas

*This simple dish of minced beef and peas in a tangy lemon sauce is both
economical and tasty.
Serve with Chapatis (page 122).*

SERVES 4 · PREPARATION TIME 15 MINUTES · COOKING TIME 1 HOUR

450 g/1 lb lean minced steak or beef
  (ground beef)
2 medium onions
2·5-cm/1-in piece fresh root ginger
2 tablespoons oil
2 cloves garlic, crushed
2 teaspoons ground coriander
1 teaspoon ground cumin
chilli powder to taste
½ teaspoon turmeric
4 cloves

4 green cardamons
4 black peppercorns
2·5-cm/1-in stick cinnamon
bay leaf
salt to taste
2–3 ripe tomatoes
100 g/4 oz (¾ cup) frozen peas
300 ml/½ pint (1¼ cups) water
4 tablespoons lemon juice
2 tablespoons chopped coriander leaves

Stir-fry the mince in a heavy-based pan over gentle heat until evenly browned.
Transfer it to a dish and set aside. Finely chop the onion and ginger. Heat the oil
in the same pan. Add the chopped ingredients and garlic and stir-fry until
golden brown, then stir in all the ground and whole spices and salt. Cook this
spice mixture for a further 3–5 minutes. Finely chop the tomatoes and add them
to the pan. Continue to cook, stirring frequently, until the tomatoes are reduced
to a pulp. Add a little water from time to time to prevent the mixture from
sticking to the bottom of the pan.

    Add the fried mince and the peas, then stir-fry for a few minutes and pour in
the water. Stir well, bring to the boil then reduce the heat, cover and cook,
stirring frequently for 30–40 minutes until the mince is cooked and all the
excess moisture has evaporated. Add the lemon juice and cook for a further 5
minutes. Transfer the Keema Mattar to a warmed dish and sprinkle it with the
chopped coriander leaves before serving.

Clockwise from the top: Bhare Baingan (page 44), Chana Dall (page 45) and
Badshahi Seekh Kebabs (page 38) with Zaffran Pullao (page 120)

Bhare Baingan
Stuffed aubergines

(Illustrated on page 42)
These small purple aubergines (eggplants) are eaten as a starter or as an accompaniment.

SERVES 4 · PREPARATION TIME 20 MINUTES · COOKING TIME 20 MINUTES

8 small aubergines (eggplants)
2 tablespoons ground coriander
1 tablespoon ground cumin
1 teaspoon garam masala (page 119)
2 teaspoons mango powder

salt to taste
chilli powder to taste
2 small onions
2–3 tablespoons oil

Wash and dry the aubergines. Carefully slit them lengthways into 4 sections held together at the stalk end. Mix all the ground spices, salt and chilli powder together and carefully stuff some of the mixture into each of the aubergines, pressing the sections back together. Peel and quarter the onions.

Heat the oil in a large frying pan (skillet), add the aubergines and onion quarters and fry over gentle heat, turning them carefully once or twice, until they are tender. Cover the pan if the fat splutters during cooking. Serve hot or cold.

Chana Dall

(Illustrated on page 42)
This vegetarian dish is also relished as an accompaniment to meat dishes.
Serve with Parathas (page 122) or poultry curries.

SERVES 4 · PREPARATION TIME 1¼ HOURS · COOKING TIME 1 HOUR

225 g/8 oz (1 cup) chana dall
1 teaspoon salt
½ teaspoon turmeric
600 ml/1 pint (2½ cups) water
1 tablespoon ghee (page 118)

1 small onion, finely chopped
1-cm/½-in piece fresh root ginger, finely
    chopped
1 teaspoon chilli powder
1 tablespoon chopped coriander leaves

Rinse the dall then soak in fresh water for 1 hour. Drain and place them in a saucepan along with the salt, turmeric and water. Bring to the boil, reduce the heat and gently simmer the dall for 30–40 minutes until they are tender and slightly creamy, and most of the water has been absorbed. Transfer them to a warmed serving dish and keep hot.

Heat the ghee, add the onion and ginger and stir-fry to a rich golden colour. Add the chilli powder, stir well and pour over the hot, cooked dall. Sprinkle with chopped coriander leaves and serve immediately.

Nepal

The memory of my brief visit to Nepal is of a country of majestic beauty
– a vision of snow-capped mountains and lush green valleys.

The people, many of them very poor, live in this harsh climate with a
kind of serenity unknown to city dwellers. Life tends to pass them by at
a very leisurely pace, and they have little regard to what is happening
in the world outside their mountain walls.

The food of the region is simple: rice and potatoes form the staple
diet with whatever vegetables that can be grown in the harsh climate of
high altitudes. Lamb, poultry and a little fish is available, and the
cooking is influenced by Chinese tastes in the northern part of the
country and Indian in the South. The curries are very similar to those of
the northern and eastern regions of India – mild in flavour, sparing in
the use of chillies, and served with a thickened sauce to be eaten with
the rice.

In this section I have included a selection of dishes which are
characteristically more Nepalese in origin than Indian.

Spicy Potato Kofta

The common potato must be one of the most versatile vegetables in the world.
So much can be done with this humble vegetable – the list is almost endless.
These potato kofta are cooked in a spicy sauce and just melt in your mouth.
Serve with plain boiled rice.

SERVES 4 · PREPARATION TIME 20 MINUTES · COOKING TIME 45 MINUTES

450 g/1 lb potatoes
25 g/1 oz (3 tablespoons) green raisins or
    sultanas (seedless white raisins)
small piece fresh root ginger
1 green chilli (chili pepper)
1 tablespoon chopped coriander leaves
4 tablespoons plain flour
oil for deep frying

2 medium onions
4 ripe tomatoes
2 tablespoons oil
$\frac{1}{2}$ teaspoon turmeric
$1\frac{1}{2}$ teaspoons ground coriander
$\frac{1}{2}$ teaspoon ground cumin
salt to taste
chilli powder to taste
750 ml/$1\frac{1}{4}$ pints (generous 3 cups) water

Scrub but do not peel the potatoes. Cook them in salted boiling water for 20–30 minutes or until soft. Meanwhile, soak the raisins in a little cold water for a few minutes then drain them and squeeze out any excess water. Finely chop the ginger and green chilli and mix them with the chopped coriander and raisins. Drain and thoroughly mash the potatoes.

Take a spoonful of potato and, with well-floured hands, shape it into a ball. Make an indent in the centre with your finger, then press a little of the raisin mixture into the centre and re-shape the potato into a smooth ball. Coat the kofta lightly in flour. Repeat until all the potato is used up.

Heat the oil for deep frying to 180 c/350 f. Carefully lower the potato kofta into the oil a few at a time and cook them until crisp and golden. Drain carefully and set aside.

Finely chop the onion and tomatoes. Heat the 2 tablespoons oil, add the onion and stir-fry until golden. Add all the spices, salt and chilli powder. Continue to stir-fry for another 2–3 minutes before adding the tomatoes and cook until they are reduced to a pulp, adding a little water if necessary. Cook the sauce until the oil begins to separate out, then pour in the water, stir until well mixed and bring it to the boil. Reduce the heat, cover the pan and simmer gently for 20 minutes, or until the sauce is reduced slightly.

Carefully add the fried potato kofta, reduce the heat and partially cover the pan. Cook the kofta gently for 10–15 minutes until they have absorbed some of the sauce and it is slightly thickened.

Nepalese Fried Fish

Freshwater fish is eaten throughout Nepal. The fish is often dried during the summer in preparation for the harsh winter months when food is scarce. This simple dish of fried fresh fish may be served as a first course or savoury snack.

SERVES 4 · PREPARATION TIME 15 MINUTES · COOKING TIME 20 MINUTES

450 g/1 lb white fish fillets
salt to taste
chilli powder to taste
1 teaspoon ground cumin
1½ teaspoons ground coriander

½ teaspoon turmeric
1 clove garlic, crushed
2 tablespoons lemon juice
4–5 tablespoons oil for frying

Skin the fish and remove any bones. Rinse and dry it on absorbent kitchen paper, then cut the flesh into 2·5-cm/1-in cubes. Mix together all the remaining ingredients except the oil and spread this paste over the pieces of fish, then leave them to marinate for 5–10 minutes.

Heat the oil, add the fish a few pieces at a time and fry them, turning carefully, until rich golden brown on all sides. Drain and serve immediately.

Chicken Curry

This simple curry is best cooked a day in advance. Leave it overnight and eat it next day when the flavour will have matured. Serve with plain boiled rice.

SERVES 4 · PREPARATION TIME 25 MINUTES · COOKING TIME 1¾ HOURS

8 small chicken portions
4 medium onions
2·5-cm/1-in piece fresh root ginger
2 cloves garlic
3 tablespoons oil
1 teaspoon turmeric

1 teaspoon chilli powder
2 teaspoons ground coriander
1 teaspoon garam masala (page 119)
salt to taste
4 tablespoons natural yogurt
600 ml/1 pint (2½ cups) water

Skin the chicken. Grind the onions, ginger and garlic to a smooth paste. Heat the oil in a pan, add the onion paste and fry it, stirring frequently, to a rich golden colour. Add a little water to prevent the mixture from sticking to the pan. Sprinkle the spices and salt over the curry, stir well and continue cooking for a few minutes. Lightly whip the yogurt and add it a little at a time. Stirring continuously, cook until most of the moisture has evaporated and the mixture is rich and brown. Add the chicken pieces and fry, turning them frequently until golden. Pour the water over the top, mix well, cover the pan and cook until the chicken is tender and the sauce has thickened – about 1 hour. Serve immediately.

Spiced Lamb Curry

Lamb and mutton are the most popular meats used in Nepalese cookery. Serve with plain boiled rice.

SERVES 4 · PREPARATION TIME 15–20 MINUTES · COOKING TIME 1¼ HOURS

450 g/1 lb tender boneless lamb	2·5-cm/1-in stick cinnamon
2 medium onions	bay leaf
25 g/1 oz (¼ cup) blanched almonds	1 black cardamom
4 ripe tomatoes	1 tablespoon chopped coriander leaves
3 tablespoons ghee (page 118) or oil	½ teaspoon turmeric
6 black peppercorns	salt to taste
1 teaspoon cumin seeds	chilli powder to taste
4 cloves	600 ml/1 pint (2½ cups) water

Cut the meat into 2·5-cm/1-in cubes. Peel and finely grate the onions, roughly chop the almonds and chop the tomatoes. Heat the ghee or oil, add the onions and stir-fry until they turn golden brown. Add the whole spices, stir-fry for a few minutes, then add the almonds, chopped coriander, meat and turmeric. Cook, stirring, until the meat is well browned. Add the tomatoes, salt and chilli powder and stir-fry until the tomatoes are reduced to a pulp. Pour in the water – it should come to about 2·5 cm/1 in over the top of the meat. Stir well, bring to the boil and reduce the heat. Cover the pan and simmer the curry gently for 45–50 minutes until the meat is tender and the sauce has thickened.

Sri Lanka

Famous for its fragrant tea plantations, surrounded by seas alive with giant lobsters, crabs and prawns, this paradise island with its swaying coconut palms abounds in exotic fruits and vegetables.

The food preferences of the country are a blend from the cultures of the several nations that have ruled there in the past – Dutch, English and Portuguese. At the same time there is a strong leaning towards the Malaysian style of cooking and Tamils, too, from South India, settling in the northern part of the island, have introduced their own eating patterns.

The curries cooked in Sri Lanka contain the usual Indian curry spices as well as the shrimp paste seasoning which is such a favourite of the Malaysians, and with the generous use of chillies, both green and red, all the food is extremely hot. You can, of course, when cooking a curry reduce the quantity of chilli powder to suit your own taste, but it is as well to be warned if you are invited to a Sri Lankan home for a meal.

But perhaps the most characteristic feature of a Sri Lankan curry is the exceptionally dark colour, totally different from the colour of an Indian curry, resulting from the custom of dry roasting the spices before grinding them. In fact, so much grinding is required in preparing a true Sir Lankan curry that you will find a hand or electric grinder an indispensable tool.

Isso Thel Dhala

Dry fried prawns

If you want to try this dish in true Sri Lankan style then you must use a large amount of chilli powder, but if you are unaccustomed to eating hot food you may damage your taste buds for quite some time! I would recommend you to use paprika to achieve the deep red colour and add just a dash of chilli powder. Serve with plain boiled rice.

SERVES 4 · PREPARATION TIME 15 MINUTES · COOKING TIME 25–30 MINUTES

2 medium onions
2 cloves garlic
2 tablespoons oil
chilli powder to taste
salt to taste
2 teaspoons paprika (paprika pepper)
$\frac{1}{4}$ teaspoon turmeric

450 g/1 lb peeled king prawns
1 teaspoon shrimp powder
6 tablespoons water
$1\frac{1}{2}$ teaspoons sugar
1 tablespoon concentrated tomato purée
 (tomato paste)

Finely chop the onions and garlic. Heat the oil in a large heavy-based frying pan (skillet), add the onion and garlic and stir-fry until transparent, soft and lightly golden. As soon as the oil begins to separate out add the chilli powder, salt, paprika and turmeric. Stirring continuously, fry this mixture for 1–2 minutes. Add the prawns and shrimp powder, mix well and fry for a further 3–4 minutes, stirring frequently to prevent the mixture sticking to the pan. Stir in the water and cook gently for 5 minutes.

Finally, stir in the sugar and tomato purée and cook, uncovered, for a few minutes until the sauce becomes a rich, dark reddish brown in colour and thickens enough to coat the prawns.

Ambul Thiyal

Fish in tamarind sauce

The authentic acidic flavour in this dish is achieved by using a bright orange fruit called goraka. Its segments are dried in the sun and turn almost black. Unfortunately, they are not widely available but tamarind pulp is an excellent substitute.
Serve with Ghee rice (page 53).

SERVES 4–6 · PREPARATION TIME 25 MINUTES · COOKING TIME 40 MINUTES

25 g/1 oz ($\frac{1}{4}$ cup) tamarind
3 tablespoons vinegar
450 g/1 lb firm white fish fillets (for example cod or haddock)
1 medium onion
small piece fresh root ginger
1 clove garlic
salt to taste
4–6 fresh or dried curry leaves

freshly ground black pepper
pinch of chilli powder
1 stalk lemon grass or thinly pared rind of $\frac{1}{2}$ lemon
2·5-cm/1-in stick cinnamon
a few fenugreek seeds
2 tablespoons oil
350 ml/12 fl oz (1$\frac{1}{2}$ cups) water

It is always best to prepare the tamarind pulp just before use. Soak the tamarind in the vinegar for 15 minutes. Squeeze it with the finger tips to loosen all the pulp, fibres and seeds, then strain it through a fine sieve, reserving the pulp and discarding the fibres and the seeds.

Skin the fish, remove any bones and rinse and pat the flesh dry. Cut it into 5-cm/2-in pieces. Finely chop the onion, ginger and garlic. Place all the ingredients, except the fish, in an enamel or stainless steel saucepan and bring to the boil. Continue to boil rapidly for a few minutes, then reduce the heat, add the fish and allow it to simmer, uncovered, for 30 minutes until the sauce has thickened and the fish is tender.

Care must be taken not to break the pieces of fish during cooking, so it is best to gently shake the pan a few times to ensure that it is well coated with the sauce. The fish may be turned over once or twice during cooking but great care must be taken in doing so. Serve piping hot.

Ghee Rice

SERVES 4 · PREPARATION TIME 40 MINUTES · COOKING TIME 35 MINUTES

275 g/10 oz (1¼ cups) long-grain rice
1 large onion
3 green cardamoms
2 tablespoons ghee (page 118)
2 cloves

1-cm/½-in stick cinnamon
900 ml/1½ pints (3¾ cups) chicken or
    beef stock
salt to taste

Rinse the rice until the water runs clear, then soak it in fresh water for at least 30 minutes. Thinly slice the onion and lightly crush the cardamoms. Heat the ghee in a large heavy-based saucepan. Add the onion and fry it to a rich golden brown. Drain the rice and add it to the onion together with the cloves, cardamoms and cinnamon. Stir-fry for a few minutes without letting the rice stick to the pan. Add the stock and salt, bring it to the boil then reduce the heat to its lowest setting and cover the pan with a tight-fitting lid. Cook, covered, for 15–20 minutes, then fluff up the rice with a fork.

Sri Lankan Curry Powder

Indian and Sri Lankan curry powders are totally different and not interchangeable. One of the characteristics of a Sri Lankan curry is the practice of roasting the spices to a rich dark brown. This increases their pungency and gives them a distinct flavour of their own.

MAKES 150–175 G/6 OZ · PREPARATION TIME 15 MINUTES

50 g/2 oz (½ cup) coriander seeds
25 g/1 oz (¼ cup) white cumin seeds
15 g/½ oz (1½ tablespoons) fennel seeds
a few fenugreek seeds
2·5-cm/1-in stick cinnamon

4–5 cloves
4–5 green cardamoms
10 fresh or dried curry leaves
½ teaspoon chilli powder

Heat a heavy-based frying pan (skillet), add the coriander seeds and, stirring continuously, dry-roast them until they are a rich dark brown in colour. Do not burn the spices or the flavour and aroma will be ruined. Remove them from the pan to a small basin. Roast the cumin, fennel and fenugreek seeds separately in the same way. Mix all the roasted and unroasted spices, curry leaves and chilli powder and grind them to a fine powder. You can store the curry powder in an airtight jar for up to a month.

Thara Padre Curry

Duck padre curry

(Illustrated on page 59)
Initially I thought this dish was a local speciality, named after one particular
'padre', but it seems that it is popular all over Sri Lanka. The distinct flavour is
due to the use of whisky as one of the ingredients.
Serve with plain boiled rice.

SERVES 8 · PREPARATION TIME 45 MINUTES · COOKING TIME 1¼–1½ HOURS

2 (1·25-kg/2½-lb) ducks or 8 duck
  portions
4 cloves garlic
3 medium onions
2·5-cm/1-in piece fresh root ginger
2·5-cm/1-in stick cinnamon
6 tablespoons Sri Lankan curry powder
  (page 53)
1 stalk lemon grass or thinly pared rind
  of ½ lemon

salt to taste
450 ml/¾ pint (scant 2 cups) thin coconut
  milk (page 119)
4 dried rampe leaves
3 tablespoons vinegar
1 tablespoon soft brown sugar
  (coffee sugar)
2 tablespoons ghee (page 118)
  or oil
3 tablespoons whisky

Joint each duck into four portions. Place the duck portions in a large heavy-based saucepan or flameproof casserole. Add all the remaining ingredients except the sugar, ghee or oil and the whisky. Bring to the boil, then reduce the heat and cover the pan with a tight-fitting lid. Simmer the duck for 50–60 minutes until it is tender. Remove the pan from the heat and carefully lift out the duck with a slotted spoon. Pat each portion dry with absorbent kitchen paper.

Heat the ghee or oil in a separate pan, add the duck pieces and fry them evenly on both sides until crisp and golden. Return the portions to the sauce, add the sugar and whisky and stir well. Bring it to the boil, reduce the heat and simmer for 10–15 minutes until all the flavours are thoroughly blended. Serve piping hot.

Harak Mas Curry

Beef curry

The most distinctive difference between an Indian beef curry and a Sri Lankan beef curry lies in the colour. The spices in this curry are roasted until very dark and this characteristic colour is imparted to the sauce and the beef. Serve with plain boiled rice and Pol Sambal (page 57).

SERVES 4 · PREPARATION TIME 15 MINUTES · COOKING TIME 1½ HOURS

450 g/1 lb braising steak (chuck steak or blade beef)
2 tablespoons oil
1 medium onion, chopped
2 teaspoons finely chopped fresh root ginger
2 cloves garlic, crushed
½ teaspoon mustard seeds
½ teaspoon turmeric
6 teaspoons Sri Lankan curry powder (page 53)
salt to taste
chilli powder to taste
2 teaspoons vinegar
2 small tomatoes, chopped
600 ml/1 pint (2½ cups) water

Cut the steak into 5-cm/2-in cubes. Heat the oil, add the onion, ginger and garlic and fry to a rich golden colour. Add the mustard seeds and continue to cook until they pop, then stir in the turmeric and curry powder. Stir-fry over low heat for 2–3 minutes before adding the salt, chilli powder and vinegar. Stir well, then add the meat and tomatoes. Ensure that the meat is well coated with the spices. Pour in the water, stir well and bring it to the boil. Reduce the heat, cover and cook the curry for 50–60 minutes until the meat is tender.

If a thicker sauce is required, at the end of the cooking time the pan may be uncovered and the sauce boiled until the required consistency is reached.

Rabu Kolle Mallung
Shredded radish leaf

The small leaves from radishes are generally discarded, yet they are a delicious accompaniment both cooked, or raw in salads.

SERVES 4 · PREPARATION TIME 10 MINUTES · COOKING TIME 15–20 MINUTES

leaves from 2 bunches red radishes
1 tablespoon oil
1 medium onion, chopped
salt to taste
chilli powder to taste

½ teaspoon turmeric
1 teaspoon shrimp powder
2 tablespoons fresh lemon juice
2 tablespoons desiccated coconut
(shredded coconut)

Wash, trim and chop the radish leaves. Heat the oil and fry the onion until golden. Add all the remaining ingredients, reduce the heat and cover the pan. Cook until the leaves are tender and most of the moisture has evaporated – about 5–10 minutes.

Elolu Kiri Hodhi
Vegetable curry

(Illustrated on page 59)
This is a basic recipe for a white curry. A whole variety of vegetables can be used: for example, potatoes, green peppers, pumpkin, marrow (summer squash) or aubergines (eggplant) and unroasted cashew nuts may be added. Serve with plain boiled rice.

SERVES 4 · PREPARATION TIME 15 MINUTES · COOKING TIME 45–50 MINUTES

1 medium onion
1 clove garlic
small piece fresh root ginger
450 g/1 lb mixed fresh vegetables in season
1 green chilli (chili pepper)
½ teaspoon turmeric
2·5-cm/1-in stick cinnamon
2 dried rampe leaves

2 stalks lemon grass or thinly pared rind of 1 small lemon
4 curry leaves
600 ml/1 pint (2½ cups) thin coconut milk (page 119)
salt to taste
150 ml/¼ pint (¾ cup) thick coconut milk (page 119)

Thinly slice the onion, garlic and ginger. Prepare the rest of the vegetables and cut them into even slices. Place the onion, garlic and ginger in a pan with the chilli, turmeric and cinnamon. Add the rampe leaves, lemon grass or rind and curry leaves. Pour over the thin coconut milk and heat gently then simmer the curry, uncovered, for 10 minutes. It is important to leave the pan uncovered to prevent the sauce from curdling.

Add the prepared vegetables and salt. Stir to mix well, then cook gently until the vegetables are tender. This will take about 20–30 minutes. Add the thick coconut milk and simmer for 5 minutes. Serve immediately.

Lunu Miris Sambal
Ground onion and chilli sambal

No matter how simple or elaborate the meal, it is not complete without the accompanying chutneys, pickles or sambals. This simply prepared sambal is very often served with just plain boiled rice.

SERVES 4 · PREPARATION TIME 15 MINUTES

5 whole dried red chillies
(chili peppers)
2 teaspoons shrimp power

1 small onion
salt to taste
1 tablespoon lemon juice

Remove the stalks from the chillies. Place all the ingredients in a liquidiser or food processor and blend them to a smooth paste. If a hotter version is required then increase the number of chillies.

Pol Sambal
Coconut sambal

(Illustrated on page 59)
A truly delicious, hot sambal which can be quickly prepared for serving with rice dishes or curries.

SERVES 4 · PREPARATION TIME 5 MINUTES

1 small onion
100 g/4 oz desiccated coconut
(1⅓ cups shredded coconut)
salt to taste

chilli powder to taste
1 tablespoon lemon juice
1 teaspoon paprika (paprika pepper)
1 tablespoon warm milk

Chop the onion finely, place it in a bowl and thoroughly mix in all the remaining ingredients. (They are traditionally mixed with the fingertips.)

Sri Lankan Roti
Sri Lankan bread

Sri Lankan rotis differ from the Indian type in that they contain fresh or desiccated coconut and can be made of wholemeal, plain or rice flour. As well as being a firm favourite for serving with curries, rotis are also a popular breakfast dish.

MAKES ABOUT 10 · PREPARATION TIME 40 MINUTES · COOKING TIME 30 MINUTES

275 g/10 oz (2½ cups) wholemeal flour
75 g/3 oz (1 cup) grated fresh or
  desiccated coconut (shredded
  coconut)

½ teaspoon salt
about 8 fl oz/250 ml (1 cup) water
ghee (page 118) or oil for frying

Mix the flour, coconut and salt in a bowl. Add the water a little at a time and bind the flour mixture together to a soft dough. Knead the dough for a few minutes until it is smooth and manageable, leaving the sides of the bowl clean. Wrap the dough in cling film or place it in a covered bowl and leave it to rest for 20 minutes.

Heat a griddle or heavy-based frying pan (skillet) and grease it lightly with the ghee or oil. Divide the dough into small portions about the size of a plum and, on a lightly floured work surface, carefully roll each piece into a circle measuring 10 cm/4 in. in diameter. Cook the roti one at a time on the hot griddle until bubbles appear on the surface. This indicates that the underside is cooked. Turn it with a spatula or fish slice and cook for a few minutes until the surface bubbles. Smear with a little ghee or oil on the top and round the edges of the roti to lightly fry it. Turn the roti over twice more, brushing a little ghee or oil on top and cook until crisp and brown on both sides.

Remove from the frying pan or griddle and keep hot while cooking the rest. Serve hot or they will lose their crisp texture if allowed to get cold.

Clockwise from the top: Thara Padre Curry (page 54), Elolu Kiri Hodhi (page 56) and Pol Sambal (page 57)

Burma

The long-standing connections that exist between India and Burma have been cemented by immigrants who have come, surprisingly, not from the neighbouring East but from the North and South of India. It was, in fact, the Marwaris from Rajasthan, Punjabis from North India and a small number of Tamils from South India who went across to settle in the rich, fertile land of Burma. The immigrants from these areas introduced the distinctive features of their own cuisines, notably their curry spices.

Native Burmese food is similar to Thai food and is not unlike that of the Chinese. Rice and fish play an important part in the diet, and fish sauce is the basic flavouring used in all dishes, including the curries. It is used in small quantities, but the taste for it has to be acquired.

During a 10-month stay in Rangoon I spent many happy hours visiting the market stalls and sampling the tasty concoctions on sale. Standing out in my memory is one particular stall, always drawing a long queue, where you could enjoy the most delicious kaukswe (egg noodles) served with a piquant chicken curry. The waiting was always well worth while. It was in Rangoon, too, that I first had a glimpse of the king-sized prawns that were made into an excellent curry.

Clockwise from the top: Thanatsone (page 68), Balachaung (page 69), Pazoon Hin (page 63) and Wetha Lone Kyaw (page 67)

Nga See Byan

Spicy fish curry

Both sea and freshwater fish form a very important part of the diet of the natives of Burma. Fish is fried, sautéed, steamed, curried, made into soups and preserved in salt.
Serve with plain boiled rice.

SERVES 4 · PREPARATION TIME 30 MINUTES · COOKING TIME 25–30 MINUTES

675 g/1½ lb firm white fish fillets
¼ teaspoon shrimp paste
1 tablespoon hot water
2 medium onions
1 clove garlic
small piece fresh root ginger
salt to taste

chilli powder to taste
½ teaspoon turmeric
1 stalk lemon grass or thinly pared rind
    of ½ lemon
2–3 tablespoons oil
2 tablespoons chopped coriander leaves

Skin the fish, remove any bones, rinse the flesh and pat it dry on absorbent kitchen paper. Cut it into 5-cm/2-in pieces. Mix the shrimp paste with the water. Place the fish pieces in a shallow dish, pour the shrimp mixture over and leave to marinate for 10–15 minutes.

Grind the onions, garlic, ginger, salt, chilli powder, turmeric and lemon grass or rind to a smooth paste. Heat the oil, add the paste and, stirring continuously, fry it to a rich golden colour or until the oil starts to separate out and the mixture leaves the sides of the pan clean.

Add the pieces of fish and cook for approximately 8–10 minutes, turning it carefully halfway through the cooking time. Transfer the curry to a warmed serving dish and serve at once sprinkled with the chopped coriander leaves.

Note: The ground onion paste for this and many of the other curries may be prepared and frozen in a small neat, tightly sealed package. It will then be ready for quickly frying and cooking with the prepared fish at a later date. It can be stored for up to 2 months in the freezer.

Pazoon Hin

Spicy prawn curry

(Illustrated on page 60)
There is nothing quite as delicious as the large prawns to be found off the
Burmese coast. They are cooked in a variety of ways, one of which is to curry
them. Large frozen prawns can be used if fresh ones are not available.
Serve with plain boiled rice and Thanatsone (page 68).

SERVES 4 · PREPARATION TIME 15 MINUTES · COOKING TIME 35–40 MINUTES

2 medium onions
2·5-cm/1-in piece fresh root ginger
2 cloves garlic
½ teaspoon chilli powder
½ teaspoon turmeric
2–3 tablespoons oil
pinch each of ground cloves, fennel and
    ground cardamom
salt to taste

1 large potato, peeled and diced
2 ripe tomatoes, peeled and chopped
150 ml/¼ pint (⅔ cup) each thin and thick
    coconut milk (page 119)
450 g/1 lb peeled king prawns
2 tablespoons chopped coriander leaves
a small bunch spring onions (scallions),
    chopped

Grind the onions, ginger and garlic to a smooth paste. Add the chilli powder
and turmeric and mix well. Heat the oil, add the onion mixture and, stirring
continuously, fry it until the oil starts to separate out and the mixture leaves
the sides of pan clean. Add the ground cloves, fennel, cardamom, salt, potato
and tomato.

Stir well, cover and cook for 8–10 minutes until the tomatoes are reduced to
a pulp. Add the thin coconut milk and simmer it gently, uncovered, for 8–10
minutes.

Finally add the prawns with the thick coconut milk. Stirring frequently,
cook the mixture, uncovered, for 3–5 minutes. Remove from the heat, add the
coriander leaves and spring onions, stir well and serve hot.

Panthe Kaukswe

Chicken curry

Panthe Kaukswe was the most memorable of my favourite dishes, tasted during my short stay in Rangoon. Our Burmese neighbour served this dish with freshly made egg noodles (kaukswe). These can be bought, dried, in most oriental food stores.

SERVES 4 · PREPARATION TIME 20–30 MINUTES · COOKING TIME 1½ HOURS

1 (1-kg/2¼-lb) chicken or
   4 chicken joints
2 medium onions
small piece fresh root ginger
2 cloves garlic
1 teaspoon shrimp paste
2 tablespoons peanut or vegetable oil
2 tablespoons sesame oil

chilli powder to taste
salt to taste
300 ml/½ pint (1¼ cups) each thin and
   thick coconut milk
1½ tablespoons chick pea flour
450 g/1 lb thin egg noodles (kaukswe) or
   Kyazan (page 67)

Cut the chicken into 8 pieces. Grind the onions, ginger, garlic and shrimp paste together to form a smooth paste. Add a little of the peanut or vegetable oil to help the grinding process.

Heat the sesame oil with the remaining peanut or vegetable oil in a large pan. Add the paste stir-fry until it is a rich golden brown. Add the chicken pieces and continue to cook, turning frequently, so that the chicken is completely coated with the spices. Add the chilli powder, salt and thin coconut milk. Stir well, then reduce the heat, cover the pan and cook the curry gently for 1 hour until the chicken is tender. Add a little hot water if the sauce becomes too thick.

When the chicken is nearly cooked, add the thick coconut milk, and stirring continuously, bring it to just below boiling point. Care must be taken to stir the sauce continuously so as to prevent it from curdling. Mix the chick pea flour to a smooth paste with a little cold water. Add it to the chicken and, again stirring continuously, cook the mixture for a further 5 minutes. There should be a fair amount of liquid in the pan, as the curry is to be eaten with thin egg or cellophane noodles.

Ametha Net Aaloo Hin

Beef and potato curry

Although this is traditionally a recipe for beef, lamb or mutton can be used instead. Other vegetables may be substituted for the potatoes.
Serve with plain boiled rice.

SERVES 4 · PREPARATION TIME 20 MINUTES · COOKING TIME 1¼ HOURS

675 g/1½ lb lean braising beef
  (chuck steak)
1 teaspoon ground cumin
1 teaspoon ground coriander
2 large onions
small bunch fresh coriander leaves,
  trimmed
2·5-cm/1-in piece fresh root ginger

2 cloves garlic
chilli powder to taste
¾ teaspoon turmeric
4 tablespoons oil
350 g/12 oz (¾ lb) potatoes, peeled and
  quartered
salt to taste
600 ml/1 pint (2½ cups) water

Trim any excess fat from the meat and cut it into 5-cm/2-in pieces. Sprinkle the ground cumin and coriander over the meat and rub them thoroughly into the cubes, then set it aside to marinate for 1–2 hours.

Grind the onions, coriander leaves, ginger, garlic, chilli powder and turmeric to a smooth paste. Heat the oil, add the paste and, stirring frequently, fry it until well browned and the oil starts to separate out.

Add the meat and, stirring frequently, cook until evenly browned and thoroughly coated with the paste mixture. Add the quartered potatoes and stir-fry for another few minutes, then add the salt and water. Stir well, bring it to the boil and reduce the heat, then cover the pan and cook the curry gently for 50–60 minutes until the meat is tender and the potatoes are cooked.

Variation Use lean, tender lamb off the leg instead of the brasing beef. Prepare the meat and substitute either 225 g/8 oz (½ lb) small button mushrooms or peeled and thickly sliced carrots instead of the potatoes. Cook and serve the curry as above. This curry freezes very well and may be stored for up to 3 months.

Wetha See Byan

Piquant pork curry

All excess fat is usually trimmed off meat before cooking; however a certain amount of pork fat is left on the meat in this dish to give it more flavour. Serve with plain boiled rice.

SERVES 4 · PREPARATION TIME 20 MINUTES · COOKING TIME 1 HOUR

450 g/1 lb fairly lean boneless pork
2 medium onions
small piece fresh root ginger
1 clove garlic
½ teaspoon turmeric
½ teaspoon chilli powder
2 tablespoons oil

¼ teaspoon shrimp paste
1 tablespoon hot water
1 stalk lemon grass, crushed or grated
   rind of ½ lemon
1–2 tablespoons tamarind juice
   (page 119)
2 tablespoons chopped coriander leaves

Remove most of the fat from the meat to leave only a very thin layer and cut it into 5-cm/2-in cubes. Grind the onions, ginger, garlic, turmeric and chilli powder to a smooth paste. Heat the oil, add the paste and, stirring frequently, fry until it is well browned and the oil starts to separate out. Add the pork and fry the meat until well browned and coated with the paste mixture. Stir the meat continuously to prevent it from sticking to the pan. Reduce the heat, cover the pan and simmer the curry gently in its own liquid for 40 minutes, or until tender. If the curry begins to dry up, add a little water to prevent the meat from sticking to the pan.

    Add the shrimp paste, water, lemon grass or lemon rind to the meat along with the tamarind juice. Stir well, and continue cooking for 5–10 minutes until all the liquid has evaporated. At this stage the oil should separate out and float to the top. Stir the curry and serve it hot, sprinkled with freshly chopped coriander leaves.

Wetha Lone Kyaw
Fried pork balls

(Illustrated on page 60)
These make a very crisp and crunchy accompaniment to curry and plain rice.
They may also be served as a starter or snack with tamarind juice or lemon
wedges. Any lean meat, poultry, fish or prawns can be used instead of the pork.

SERVES 4 · PREPARATION TIME 15 MINUTES · COOKING TIME 30 MINUTES

450 g/1 lb lean boneless pork
1 medium onion
1 green chilli (chili pepper)
small bunch coriander leaves, trimmed
1 clove garlic, crushed
¼ teaspoon turmeric

salt to taste
50 g/2 oz plain flour (½ cup
   all-purpose flour)
4 tablespoons oil
small bunch of coriander leaves,
   trimmed and washed

Mince the pork. Finely chop the onion, green chilli and coriander leaves and
mix them into the pork together with the garlic, turmeric and salt. Roll the
meat mixture into walnut-sized balls and coat each with a little flour. Heat the
oil in a frying pan (skillet) and cook the meatballs a few at a time, turning them
carefully until they are crisp and golden. Drain on absorbent kitchen paper,
then pile the Wetha Lone Kyaw in small bowls. Garnish them with a few sprigs
of coriander and serve hot.

Kyazan
Cellophane noodles

These transparent noodles are found on the food stalls in the market places of
Rangoon. Serve them with Panthe Kaukswe (page 64).

SERVES 4 · COOKING TIME 25 MINUTES

1 teaspoon salt
1·75 litres/3 pints (7½ cups) water

225 g/8 oz (½ lb) cellophane noodles

Salt the water and bring it to the boil in a large saucepan. Lower the noodles
into the water and cook them rapidly, uncovered, for about 20 minutes. Drain
and serve them hot.

A whole variety of accompaniments are served with the noodles such as
finely sliced onions and spring onions (scallions); finely chopped coriander
leaves; crisp fried noodles, broken into small pieces; dry chillies (chili
peppers), crisply fried, and lemon wedges.

Ohn Htamin

Coconut rice

As in other South East Asian countries, rice forms the staple diet of the Burmese people. No matter how elaborate or simple the rest of the meal, the cook's expertise is evident in light, pure white, fluffy rice. In Burma, long-grain rice is washed in several changes of water until all the excess starch is removed and the water runs clear.

SERVES 4 · PREPARATION TIME 2–3 MINUTES · COOKING TIME 25 MINUTES

450 g/1 lb (2 cups) long-grain rice
1½ teaspoons salt

1 litre/1¾ pints (4¼ cups) thin coconut
milk (page 119)

Wash the rice in several changes of water. Mix it with the salt and coconut milk in a saucepan, bring it to the boil, then reduce the heat. Stir well, cover the pan and cook the rice gently for about 20 minutes until it is tender and all the liquid has been absorbed.

It is important not to lift the lid during cooking as the steam will escape and the rice may turn soggy. Serve hot with any meat or vegetable curry and its other accompaniments.

Thanatsone

Mixed vegetable salad

(Illustrated on page 60)
This is a truly delicious, crunchy salad with the subtle flavour of lightly roasted sesame seeds. A variety of vegetables can be used but the expertise lies in cutting them into thin julienne strips, then blanching them for just a minute to retain their crispness.

SERVES 4 · PREPARATION TIME 25 MINUTES · COOKING TIME 10 MINUTES

450 g/1 lb finely sliced mixed
   vegetables, for example carrots,
   courgettes (zucchini), bean sprouts,
   cucumber, cabbage, French beans and
   spring onions (scallions)
salt to taste
2 medium onions

1 tablespoon oil
2 teaspoons light sesame oil
2 cloves garlic, crushed
¼ teaspoon turmeric
1 tablespoon white vinegar
2 tablespoons sesame seeds

Prepare the vegetables and cut them into thin julienne strips. Blanch them, uncovered, in lightly salted, rapidly boiling water for 1–2 minutes. Drain and rinse them in cold running water to prevent any further cooking. Thinly slice the onions. Heat the two oils together in a frying pan (skillet), add the onion and garlic and stir-fry until they are crisp and golden. Add the turmeric and cook it for a few seconds. Remove the pan from the heat and stir the onion mixture for a minute. Mix the drained vegetables in a serving bowl, add the fried onion and garlic and a little of the cooking oil, then pour in the vinegar and a little salt if necessary. Lightly toss the salad to mix in the dressing.

Wipe the excess fat from the frying pan, place it over high heat and add the sesame seeds. Stirring continuously, dry roast them to a golden brown. Care must be taken not to burn the seeds or they will become bitter. Remove the seeds from the pan and allow them to cool, then sprinkle them over the vegetable salad. Serve with any meat curry and plain boiled rice.

Balachaung

(Illustrated on page 60)
Balachaung is a popular classic Burmese accompaniment made of fried shrimp powder. It is served with plain boiled rice or rice and curry and keeps well, covered, in the refrigerator for a few weeks.

SERVES 4–6 · PREPARATION TIME 5 MINUTES · COOKING TIME 15 MINUTES

1 medium onion	$\frac{1}{4}$ teaspoon shrimp paste
5 cloves garlic	2 tablespoons vinegar
3 tablespoons peanut oil	salt to taste
50 g/2 oz shrimp powder	chilli powder to taste

Peel and thinly slice the onion and garlic. Heat the oil and fry the onion and garlic until golden brown. Remove it from the pan and drain on absorbent kitchen paper, then set aside.

Add the shrimp powder to the oil in the pan and fry it for 5 minutes, stirring continuously. Mix the shrimp paste with the vinegar, add the salt and chilli powder and add it to the fried shrimp powder. Stirring well, cook for a further few minutes until the vinegar evaporates and the mixture is dry.

Remove the pan from the heat, add the crisp onion and garlic slices and mix thoroughly. Cool and store in an airtight container for up to a month.

Thailand

My first introduction to Thai food was at the Expo 70 exhibition in Japan, where a friend from the Thai pavilion a few doors away taught me in her tiny kitchen to make exquisite flowers carved out of various fruits and vegetables. She used to spend hours with tremendous patience producing these concoctions.

This patience and devotion to the details of presentation is the hallmark of Thai cooking. Be it a simple meal or a grand banquet, the housewife will take equal care and pride in presenting decorative dishes. Rice and fish are the staple diet of the people, and as in the neighbouring South East Asian countries Thais like to add a fish paste to all their dishes to enhance the flavour.

There are two very distinct types of curry, one green and the other red, according to the colour of the paste which has been made from either fresh green or red chillies with a whole lot of other ingredients. As with all their cooking, great care is taken in making a curry and it is served with rice and a large selection of side dishes — as many as the cook has time to prepare. The Thais are not too particular about the temperature of the food, but the rice must be served piping hot, so it is advisable to cook this at the last minute.

Krung Kaeng

Curry paste – red and green

Red and green curry pastes form the basis of the Thai curries. Fresh red or green chillies (chili peppers) are used to make the pastes and they can be stored in airtight containers in the refrigerator for up to a week.

MAKES ABOUT 225 G/8 OZ · PREPARATION TIME 5–10 MINUTES

2 large fresh red or green chillies
  (chili peppers)
small bunch fresh coriander with leaves,
  stems and roots
1 small onion
1 clove garlic
6–8 whole black peppercorns
1 teaspoon shrimp paste

½ teaspoon each of turmeric, cumin seeds
  and salt
1 teaspoon coriander seeds
1 tablespoon oil
½ teaspoon loas powder – optional
1 teaspoon grated lemon rind
¼ teaspoon paprika (paprika pepper) for
  red curry paste

Remove the stalks and seeds from the chillies. Wash the coriander thoroughly to remove any grit and dry it on absorbent kitchen paper. Roughly chop the onion, chillies, coriander and garlic. Grind all the ingredients together to make a smooth paste.

Kaeng Phet Kung

Prawns in red curry sauce

Prawns of all sizes are widely available all over South East Asia; in fact they come from as far off as the Bay of Bengal. Naturally, there are many different dishes using this delicious shellfish and frozen prawns may be substituted for fresh ones. This dish can be prepared in advance and thoroughly reheated before serving. It also freezes well. Serve hot with fluffy white rice.

SERVES 4 · PREPARATION TIME 30 MINUTES · COOKING TIME 30 MINUTES

6 teaspoons red curry paste (page 71)
450 ml/¾ pint (scant 2 cups) thin coconut
  milk (page 119)

salt to taste
450 g/1 lb peeled prawns

Mix the curry paste with the coconut milk and salt in a large saucepan. Stirring continuously, heat it to simmering point but take care not to let it boil as it will curdle. As soon as the sauce thickens slightly, add the prawns and cook them uncovered for about 15–20 minutes, stirring frequently.

Kaeng Khieu Wan Pla
Fish in green curry sauce

(Illustrated on page 77)
Both freshwater and sea fish are found in abundance all over Thailand. Both types are often steamed then fried, made into paste and curried. Many dishes combine both Indian and Chinese cooking techniques.

SERVES 4 · PREPARATION TIME 20 MINUTES · COOKING TIME 30–40 MINUTES

450 g/1 lb white fish fillets
600 ml/1 pint (2½ cups) thin coconut milk
  (page 119)
6 teaspoons green curry paste (page 71)
salt to taste

a few citrus leaves – optional
1 teaspoon fish sauce – optional
1 green chilli (chili pepper) – optional
1 tablespoon freshly chopped basil

Skin the fish, remove any bones, then cut it into 5-cm/2-in pieces. Pour the coconut milk into a heavy-based saucepan, mix in the green curry paste and, stirring continuously, heat it gently without boiling. Do not allow the milk to boil as it will curdle. Add the fish, salt, citrus leaves (if used) and fish sauce, reduce the heat and allow the curry to simmer gently for 20–25 minutes until the fish is tender.

Finally, remove the stalks from the chilli (if used), then chop and add it to the curry with the basil. Continue cooking for another few minutes, then serve hot with plain boiled rice.

Note: To skin fish fillets, lay them flat, skin side down, on a board or clean work surface. Use a sharp knife and hold the fish by the tail end, then cut between the flesh and the skin, holding the knife at a slight angle to the surface and working from the tail towards the head with the knife pointing away from you.

Kaeng Khieu Wan Pet

Duck with green curry sauce

The versatility of green curry paste is endless – it can be used in all kinds of meat and poultry dishes. Fresh coriander and basil enhance both the colour and flavour of this excellent dish.
Serve with plain boiled rice.

SERVES 4 · PREPARATION TIME 30 MINUTES · COOKING TIME 1–1½ HOURS

1 (1·5-kg/3¼-lb) duck
450 ml/¾ pint (scant 2 cups) thin coconut milk (page 119)
3 tablespoons green curry paste (page 71)
3–4 citrus leaves – optional

salt to taste
1–2 fresh green chillies (chili peppers)
1 tablespoon fish sauce – optional
300 ml/½ pint (1¼ cups) thick coconut milk (page 119)
small bunch basil or coriander leaves

Cut the duck into eight portions. Heat the thin coconut milk in a large saucepan to just below boiling point but do not allow it to boil. Add the duck, reduce the heat and simmer it gently for 15–20 minutes. Stir frequently to prevent the sauce from sticking to the pan.

Remove from the heat and strain off about 175 ml/6 fl oz (¾ cup) of the cooking liquid into another saucepan. Stir the green curry paste into this until the mixture is smooth and cook over medium heat until all the milk evaporates and the curry paste is well cooked. Stir continuously to prevent it from sticking to the pan. The oil will separate out at this stage and the paste should be fried for another few minutes. Add the rest of the cooking liquid from the duck, straining it over a little at a time, and continue to cook, stirring continuously, until the sauce thickens slightly and the oil separates out.

Add the partly cooked duck, citrus leaves and salt, chillies (if used), and fish sauce. Bring the mixture to boiling point, stirring continuously, add the thick coconut milk, reduce the heat and allow the mixture to simmer gently, covered, until the duck is tender and the sauce has thickened slightly – about 1 hour. Roughly chop the basil or coriander leaves and add to the sauce, then mix in thoroughly and serve hot.

Kaeng Masaman
Muslim curry

The spices used in this curry are very similar to those found in Indian ones with the addition of shrimp paste and lemon grass.
Serve with plain boiled rice.

SERVES 4 · PREPARATION TIME 30 MINUTES · COOKING TIME 1½ HOURS

2 tablespoons oil
5–6 whole black peppercorns
3 green cardamoms
2·5-cm/1-in stick cinnamon
small pinch each of ground nutmeg and
　ground mace
3–4 cloves
6 teaspoons coriander seeds
1 teaspoon cumin seeds
4 dried red chillies (chili peppers)
2 medium onions
2·5-cm/1-in piece fresh root ginger

3 cloves garlic
½ teaspoon shrimp paste
salt to taste
1 tablespoon finely chopped lemon grass
　or thinly pared rind of ½ lemon
900 ml/1½ pints (3¾ cups) thick coconut
　milk (page 119)
1 kg/2¼ lb braising steak (chuck steak) or
　lean lamb, cubed
4 tablespoons tamarind juice (page 119)
2 tablespoons lemon juice
1½ teaspoons sugar

Rub a little oil over a large heavy-based frying pan (skillet). Place all the dry spices for the curry paste in it and roast them over gentle heat until they begin to pop and change colour. As they cook they will give off a pungent aroma. Remove from the pan and cool, then grind them to a fine powder.

　Finely chop the chillies, onions, ginger and garlic. Heat the remaining oil in the same pan. Add the onion, ginger, garlic, chilli, shrimp paste and salt, then stir-fry until soft. Add this mixture to the ground spices and once again grind or liquidise the mixture to a smooth paste. Mix the lemon grass into this paste.

　Heat the coconut milk to just below boiling point in a large saucepan. Add the meat and gently simmer for 50–60 minutes until it is tender, then carefully remove it and set it aside. Allow the sauce to simmer until slightly thickened. Mix in the curry paste and cook for a few minutes, stirring continuously. Return the meat to the pan, mix well and cook until the sauce is very thick. Just before serving add the tamarind juice, lemon juice and sugar. Stir well and serve hot with boiled rice.

Khao Phat Prik

Chilli fried rice

(Illustrated on page 77)
Although steamed rice is most commonly eaten at every meal, certain well-flavoured rice dishes are also eaten. These will often include meat, fish, shellfish or eggs to make them a complete meal.

SERVES 4 · PREPARATION TIME 20 MINUTES · COOKING TIME 45–50 MINUTES

450 g/1 lb (2 cups) long-grain rice
salt to taste
1 medium onion
1 green and 1 red chilli (chili pepper)
3 tablespoons oil
1 tablespoon red curry paste (page 71)

100 g/4 oz (¼ lb) lean boneless pork
225 g/8 oz (½ lb) peeled prawns
1 tablespoon fish sauce – optional
3 tablespoons finely chopped spring onion (scallions)
2 tablespoons chopped coriander leaves

Rinse and drain the rice. Place it in a large saucepan with enough water to cover it to a depth of 2·5 cm/1 in. Add salt to taste, bring it to the boil, reduce the heat and cover closely. Simmer for about 20 minutes until all the water has been absorbed and the rice is tender.

Finely chop the onion. Remove the stalk and seeds from the chillies and chop them finely. Heat 2 tablespoons of the oil in a large frying pan (skillet) or wok, add the onion and chillies and stir-fry until they are soft. Stir in the curry paste and, stirring continuously, fry the mixture until the oil separates out.

Finely chop the pork and halve any large prawns. Stir-fry these together in the remaining oil in a separate pan until cooked, lower the heat then add the rice. Leave the pan over very gentle heat until the rice is heated through. Thoroughly mix in the fish sauce and a little salt, then add the spring onions and chopped coriander leaves and serve immediately.

Nam Prik

Thai shrimp sauce

(Illustrated on opposite page)
*Nam Prik, this extensively used shrimp sauce, is as common in Thai cooking as
soy sauce is in Chinese cuisine. It is delicious as a dip with raw or lightly boiled
vegetables (and even edible flowers), fish, shellfish or hard-boiled eggs.*

SERVES 4 · PREPARATION TIME 30 MINUTES

1 tablespoon dried shrimps
½ teaspoon shrimp paste
2 cloves garlic
1½ teaspoons ground, dried red chillies
  (chili peppers)

1½ teaspoons molasses or black treacle
1 tablespoon soy sauce
1 tablespoon lemon juice
6 teaspoons water

Thoroughly wash the dried shrimps, drain and soak them in fresh cold water
for 15–20 minutes. Rinse them and set aside. Wrap the shrimp paste in a small
piece of cooking foil and place it under a hot grill for a minute on each side.
Blend all the ingredients together in a liquidiser to make a sauce, adding a little
extra water if it is too thick.

Serve in a small bowl with the prepared vegetables, fish or eggs arranged on
plates alongside.

Clockwise from the top: Khao Phat Prik (page 75), Kaeng Khieu Wan Pla
(page 72) and Nam Prik

Yam Tang Kwa
Cucumber salad

This is a cucumber salad with a difference.

SERVES 4 · PREPARATION TIME 15 MINUTES

½ cucumber
1 medium onion
2 tablespoons lemon juice
1 tablespoon shrimp powder

salt to taste
1 fresh red chilli (chili pepper), finely
   chopped

Peel and coarsely grate both the cucumber and the onion, then mix them with the remaining ingredients and serve.

Chilli sambal

This sambal is hot enough to bring tears to your eyes!

SERVES 4 · PREPARATION TIME 10 MINUTES

3–4 fresh red chillies
   (chili peppers)

3 tablespoons lime juice
salt to taste

Grind the ingredients together into a very smooth thin paste and serve it in small quantities. This sambal keeps well for up to a week in a screw-topped jar in the refrigerator.

From the top: Sambal Tumis (page 87), Nasi Kunyit (page 87) and Gulai Tumis (page 83)

Malaysia and Singapore

Malaysia, a country similar to its neighbours with its lush green vegetation and rubber plantations, has a lot to offer the gourmet. Many immigrants from other Asian nations such as India, Sri Lanka, China and Indonesia have settled there, bringing with them their own ingredients and style of cooking. With such a cosmopolitan population, it is sometimes difficult to trace the origin of certain dishes because each community has borrowed something from the other and the mixture of influences, Muslim, Hindu and Chinese, is reflected in the eating patterns of the country.

Because of various religious taboos certain foods are forbidden to different communities – pork to the Muslims, though the Chinese use it extensively, and beef to the Hindus, many of whom are vegetarian. The most popular meats are lamb, mutton and poultry and everyone eats plenty of fish which, together with rice, forms the staple diet.

Malaysian curries are very similar to those of Indonesia and are served with a variety of side dishes such as sambals, pickles, and hot chilli sauces. Peanut oil is widely used and much of the cooking is done with it.

Sambal Ikan

Whole fish sambal

Sambals are similar to the curries brought by the immigrant Indians. All the curry spices are used to give them their distinct flavour. As with the curry powder or paste, the sambal paste can be prepared in advance and stored in a container in the refrigerator for up to a week.
Serve with plain boiled rice.

SERVES 4 · PREPARATION TIME 25–30 MINUTES · COOKING TIME 35–40 MINUTES

675 g/1½ lb whole grey mullet
25 g/1 oz cornflour (¼ cup cornstarch)
4 tablespoons coconut oil
2 medium onions
8 fresh red chillies or 6 dried red chillies
   (chili peppers)
1 teaspoon turmeric
1 tablespoon coriander seeds

½ teaspoon fennel seeds
½ teaspoon brown mustard seeds
4 tablespoons peanut oil
250 ml/8 fl oz (1 cup) thick coconut milk
   (page 119)
2–3 fresh lime leaves
salt to taste

Gut, descale and rinse the fish thoroughly in cold water. Dry it carefully on absorbent kitchen paper. Using a sharp knife, make several 7·5 to 10-cm/3 to 4-in slits on both sides of the fish, cutting right through to the bone. Dust the skin of the fish with the cornflour. Heat the coconut oil in a heavy-based frying pan (skillet) and fry the fish, turning once, until crisp and golden brown on both sides and cooked through. Carefully lift the fish out of the pan and drain it on absorbent kitchen paper. Set aside and keep hot.

Finely chop the onions, remove the stalks and seeds from the chillies and chop them finely. Grind the dry spices to a powder. Mix the onion and chillies with this powder and, adding the peanut oil a little at a time, grind the mixture to a thick paste. Transfer this paste to a wok or heavy-based frying pan (skillet) and, stirring frequently, fry until it turns brown. Take great care to ensure that the spices do not burn. The quantity of peanut oil should be sufficient to prevent the spices from drying out.

Carefully add the coconut milk, lime leaves and salt. Stir the mixture as it thickens and stand well back from the pan in case it splutters. Carefully add the fish to the pan, spooning the sauce over it, and cook, uncovered for 10–15 minutes until the fish absorbs some of the sauce and most of the liquid has evaporated.

Gulai Ikan

Simple fish curry

This very basic fish curry is cooked in coconut milk instead of water.
Serve with plain boiled rice.

SERVES 4 · PREPARATION TIME 20 MINUTES · COOKING TIME 45–50 MINUTES

small piece tamarind
450 g/1 lb cod steaks
2 medium onions
1 clove garlic
small piece fresh root ginger
6 teaspoons coriander seeds
½ teaspoon fennel seeds
¼ teaspoon cumin seeds
½ teaspoon turmeric

2 dried red chillies (chili peppers)
125 ml/4 fl oz (½ cup) thick coconut milk
  (page 119)
1 stalk lemon grass or thinly pared rind
  of ½ lemon
150 ml/¼ pint (⅔ cup) thin coconut milk
  (page 119)
salt to taste

Soak the tamarind for 15 minutes in warm water to cover. Squeeze out and reserve all the juice. Rinse the fish steaks and pat them dry with absorbent kitchen paper. Roughly chop the onions, garlic and ginger. Grind the dry spices to a powder then add the onion, garlic and ginger and continue to grind until a thick paste is formed. Gradually stir in the thick coconut milk.

Crush the lemon grass or finely chop the lemon rind and place it in a saucepan with the paste. Bring to the boil, stirring frequently, then reduce the heat and let the mixture simmer for about 10 minutes, stirring continuously. At this stage add the thin coconut milk, reserved tamarind juice and salt. Continue to stir the mixture, bring it back to the boil and cook for a few minutes.

Add the fish steaks and cook, uncovered, for a further 15–20 minutes until the fish is tender.

Gulai Tumis

Sour fish curry

(Illustrated on page 78)
Tamarind complements the flavour of most fish and is used in this dish with a combination of shrimp paste (blachan) and French beans.
Serve with plain boiled rice.

SERVES 4 · PREPARATION TIME 10–15 MINUTES · COOKING TIME 30 MINUTES

2 medium onions
1 dried red chilli (chili pepper)
2 stalks lemon grass or thinly pared rind
    of ½ lemon
½ teaspoon shrimp paste
1 teaspoon turmeric
1½ teaspoons loas powder – optional
2 cloves garlic

2 tablespoons oil
100 g/4 oz (¼ lb) French beans, fresh or
    thawed
300 ml/½ pint (1¼ cups) tamarind juice
    (page 119)
salt to taste
450 g/1 lb white fish steaks – cod, rock
    salmon or grey mullet

Finely chop the onions. Grind the chilli, lemon grass (or lemon rind), shrimp paste, turmeric, laos powder, onions and garlic together to a fine paste. Heat the oil in a frying pan (skillet) and add the paste. Stirring frequently, fry it until the oil separates out. Trim the French beans and cut them into 5-cm/2-in pieces. Stir-fry them with the paste for 3–4 minutes, then carefully add the tamarind juice and salt, standing back as it may splutter, and stir until the mixture is well blended. Bring to the boil, reduce the heat then cover and simmer for a few minutes. Carefully lower the fish steak into the sauce, cover the pan and cook gently for 8–10 minutes or until the fish is tender and has absorbed some of the sauce.

Gulai Ayam
Chicken curry

This rich, creamy chicken curry, like so many others from this region, uses shrimp paste for additional flavour. It can be prepared well in advance and thoroughly reheated before serving.
Serve with plain boiled rice.

SERVES 4 · PREPARATION TIME 25 MINUTES · COOKING TIME 1 HOUR

1 (1-kg/2¼-lb) chicken
2 tablespoons coriander seeds
1½ teaspoons fennel seeds
2 cloves
2·5-cm/1-in stick cinnamon
1 teaspoon cumin seeds
¾ teaspoon turmeric
chilli powder to taste
2 medium onions
2 cloves garlic

small piece fresh root ginger
1 stalk lemon grass or thinly pared rind
of ½ lemon
5 tablespoons oil
300 ml/½ pint (1¼ cups) thick coconut
milk (page 119)
450 ml/¾ pint (scant 2 cups) thin coconut
milk (page 119)
salt to taste
¼ teaspoon shrimp paste

Cut the chicken into 8 pieces. Grind the whole spices to a fine powder and add the turmeric and chilli powder. Grate the onions and squeeze any excess moisture out of the resulting pulp. Finely chop the garlic, ginger and lemon grass or lemon rind.

Heat the oil in a large heavy-based saucepan. Add all the ingredients except for the chicken pieces and thick and thin coconut milk. Stir-fry until aromatic and glossy in appearance. Add half the thick coconut milk to make a thick sauce. Arrange the chicken in the pan and turn it in the sauce so that each piece is well coated with the spice mixture. Add the thin coconut milk, salt and shrimp paste, stirring to blend the ingredients together. Cover the pan, reduce the heat and cook for 45–50 minutes until the chicken is tender. Check the sauce during cooking and add a little water if it begins to dry up. Add the remaining thick coconut milk to the curry, stir gently and heat through for a few minutes before serving.

Gulai Daging Lembu
Beef curry

Beef or mutton are more widely eaten than pork. In this curry the meat is marinated in the ground paste for several hours before cooking to absorb the full flavour of the spices.

SERVES 4 · PREPARATION TIME 3½–4½ HOURS · COOKING TIME 1¼ HOURS

1 tablespoon coriander seeds
1 tablespoon fennel seeds
1 teaspoon cumin seeds
4 cloves
¾ teaspoon turmeric
pinch of nutmeg
2·5-cm/1-in stick cinnamon
chilli powder to taste
450 g/1 lb braising steak (chuck steak)
2 medium onions
small piece fresh root ginger

2 cloves garlic
4 tablespoons oil
300 ml/½ pint (1¼ cups) thin coconut milk (page 119)
1 stalk lemon grass or thinly pared rind of ½ lemon
150 ml/¼ pint (⅔ cup) tamarind juice (page 119)
300 ml/½ pint (1¼ cups) thick coconut milk (page 119)
salt to taste

Grind together the powdered, dry and whole spices to a fine powder then add a little water and mix well to a smooth paste. Trim any excess fat from the meat and cut it into 2·5-cm/1-in cubes. Mix the paste and meat together, then cover and leave it to marinate for 3–4 hours. The longer the meat is allowed to marinate the better the flavour.

Mince the onions, ginger and garlic together. Heat the oil in a heavy-based saucepan, add the onion mixture and stir-fry until it is a rich golden colour. Add the marinated meat with all the paste and continue to stir-fry for a minute. Stir in the thin coconut milk and lemon grass and heat through gently. Cover the pan and reduce the heat, then allow it to simmer gently for 50–60 minutes until the meat is tender.

Reduce the heat to the lowest setting, add tamarind juice and thick coconut milk and heat it through gently without allowing the mixture to boil. Finally add salt to taste, stir well and serve hot.

Sayur Masak Lemak

Vegetable curry

One characteristic of both vegetarian and non-vegetarian curries of this region is the use of thick and thin coconut milk.
Serve with Nasi Kunyit (page 87).

SERVES 4 · PREPARATION TIME 15 MINUTES · COOKING TIME 30 MINUTES

1 medium onion
1 clove garlic
1 green chilli (chili pepper)
½ teaspoon shrimp paste
½ teaspoon turmeric
150 ml/¼ pint (⅔ cup) thin coconut milk
  (page 119)

1 large potato
450 g/1 lb green or white cabbage
salt to taste
150 ml/¼ pint (⅔ cup) thick coconut milk
  (page 119)
1 tablespoon lemon juice

Finely chop the onion, garlic and green chilli and place them in a large heavy-based saucepan along with the shrimp paste, turmeric and thin coconut milk. Heat gently to simmering point. Peel and dice the potato, add it to the pan and cook for 8–10 minutes until the potato is half cooked.

Coarsely shred the cabbage and add it to the curry with the salt. Mix all the ingredients together well and cook for a few minutes. Add the thick coconut milk and cook for a further 10 minutes, stirring occasionally, until the cabbage is tender. Add the lemon juice just before serving.

Nasi Kunyit
Yellow rice

(Illustrated on page 78)
This spiced rice dish is occasionally served with Malaysian curries.

SERVES 4 · PREPARATION TIME 10 MINUTES · COOKING TIME 25 MINUTES

450 g/1 lb (2 cups) short-grain or
    pudding rice
450 ml/¾ pint (scant 2 cups) water
½ teaspoon salt
1 clove garlic, crushed
½ teaspoon turmeric

1 rampe leaf
¼ teaspoon freshly ground black pepper
300 ml/½ pint (1¼ cups) thin coconut milk
    (page 119)
1 onion, sliced
2 tablespoons oil

Rinse and drain the rice, then place it in a saucepan along with the water, salt, garlic, turmeric, rampe leaf and pepper. Bring it to the boil, reduce the heat and cover the pan tightly, then simmer for 10 minutes until the rice is half cooked. Heat the coconut milk and mix it into the rice carefully, using a fork. Re-cover the pan and cook gently for a further 10 minutes.

Separate the onion slices into rings and fry them in the oil until crisp and golden. Drain and sprinkle them over the cooked rice.

Sambal Tumis
Fried condiment

(Illustrated on page 78)
Sambals are an important part of the meal. They are generally very hot but this accompaniment is slightly milder.

SERVES 4 · PREPARATION TIME 5 MINUTES · COOKING TIME 15 MINUTES

1 small onion
1 tablespoon chilli powder
2 tablespoons molasses or soft brown
    sugar (coffee sugar)

salt to taste
1–2 tablespoons peanut oil
2 teaspoons tamarind juice (page 119)
1 tablespoon peeled prawns

Grate the onion and squeeze any excess moisture out of the pulp. Mix in the chilli powder, molasses or sugar and salt. Heat the oil, add the onion mixture and stir-fry until it leaves the sides of the pan clean. Add the tamarind juice and prawns and cook the mixture until it starts to bubble. Serve immediately.

Indonesia

With its thousands of large and small islands, Indonesia has often been referred to as a bejewelled necklace hung between Australia and the mainland of South East Asia. Some of the islands are too small even to have a name.

Like Malaysia, Indonesia carries the legacy of a mixture of races and cultures, Indian, Chinese, English, Portuguese and Dutch, and this is reflected in the varied food customs and preferences. As the Dutch stayed the longest their influence is very strong. Scenically, Indonesia is very lush with a higher than average rainfall, and the vegetation has a growing will of its own. Rice is the staple diet of the people, and tropical fruits and vegetables abound. Along the coasts there are plentiful fish and shellfish.

Because of the influx of settlers, the cuisine is varied and interesting. The Indians brought with them their curry spices and over the years the local people have developed curries with a distinctive flavour of their own, using such additions as lemon grass and dried shrimp paste, a favourite ingredient among the people of South East Asia.

Indonesian cooking is often regarded as the 'haute cuisine' of South East Asia. Hot with chillies and rather oily, it is nevertheless very subtly flavoured with the free use of ground spices and coconut milk, both thick and thin. Much of the food is stir-fried, which helps to achieve this delicacy of flavour.

Gulai Cumi-Cumi

Piquant squid curry

(Illustrated on the back cover)
Squid requires lengthy preparation but it is well worth it — particularly for this dish where the piquancy of tamarind water or lemon juice is combined with the subtle flavour of the creamy coconut milk. It is one of my favourite dishes. Serve with plain boiled rice and Sambal Goreng Udang Asam (page 99).

SERVES 4 · PREPARATION TIME 40 MINUTES · COOKING TIME 20 MINUTES

350g/12 oz ($\frac{3}{4}$ lb) fresh squid
1 medium onion
small piece fresh root ginger
2 brazil nuts
1 teaspoon shrimp paste
salt to taste

chilli powder to taste
300 ml/$\frac{1}{2}$ pint (1$\frac{1}{4}$ cups) thin coconut milk (page 119)
3 tablespoons tamarind juice (page 119)
$\frac{1}{2}$ teaspoon muscovado sugar

Clean and gut the squid, removing the head and the ink sac. Use a little salt to rub off all the spotted skin and wash the inside thoroughly, then cut each one into bite-sized pieces.

Finely chop the onion and the root ginger and grate the brazil nuts. Mix these ingredients together in a saucepan with the shrimp paste, salt and chilli powder. Pour in the coconut milk and heat the mixture almost to boiling point, stirring continuously. Let the sauce simmer gently for a few minutes until it thickens slightly. Add the washed and drained pieces of squid, stir well and simmer gently, uncovered, for 6–8 minutes. Finally add the tamarind juice and sugar, stir thoroughly and simmer for 1–2 minutes before serving.

Gule Ikan

Piquant fish curry

*Each of the many Indonesian islands has in turn contributed its own speciality
to the cuisine of the country. This dish comes from Sumatra.
Serve with plain boiled rice and Bawang Goreng (page 98).*

SERVES 4 · PREPARATION TIME 30 MINUTES · COOKING TIME 40 MINUTES

4 small red mullet
salt
4–5 tablespoons tamarind juice
  (page 119)
2 medium onions
½ teaspoon turmeric
1 teaspoon laos powder – optional
chilli powder to taste

1 stalk lemon grass or thinly pared rind
  of ½ lemon
1 tablespoon oil
350 ml/12 fl oz (1½ cups) thick coconut
  milk (page 119)
salt to taste
3 tablespoons lemon juice

Thoroughly clean, rinse and descale the fish. Pat them dry on absorbent
kitchen paper. Make a few shallow incisions on both sides of each fish,
sprinkle them with a little salt and rub in the tamarind juice. Cover and allow to
marinate for 15–20 minutes. Meanwhile, roughly chop the onions and grind
them to a smooth paste with the turmeric, loas and chilli powder. Finely chop
the lemon grass or rind.

Heat the oil and stir-fry the paste until golden brown. Add the coconut milk
and the lemon grass. Heat the mixture to just below boiling point, stirring
continuously. Carefully lower the fish into the sauce and simmer uncovered
for 30 minutes until they are tender. Turn them once or twice to ensure that
they are thoroughly cooked. Add the salt and continue to cook for another few
minutes before stirring in the lemon juice.

Kalio Ajam

Subtle chicken curry

This quick curry is easy to prepare and should be served with plain boiled rice and Pisang Goreng (page 98).

SERVES 4 · PREPARATION TIME 30 MINUTES · COOKING TIME 1–1¼ HOURS

1 (1-kg/2¼-lb) chicken
2 medium onions
2·5-cm/1-in piece fresh root ginger
2 cloves garlic
chilli powder to taste
salt to taste
½ teaspoon turmeric

5 macadamia nuts
750–900 ml/1¼–1½ pints (3–3¾ cups) thin coconut milk (page 119)
1 stalk lemon grass
2–3 citrus leaves
2 tablespoons lemon juice

Cut the chicken into eight pieces. Roughly chop the onions and ginger and grind them to a fine paste with the garlic, chilli powder, salt, turmeric and nuts. Add a little of the coconut milk to moisten the paste.

Pour the remaining coconut milk into a saucepan, add the ground onion mixture and stir well to mix the ingredients. Chop the lemon grass and sprinkle it over the coconut milk together with the citrus leaves. Heat the mixture gently, stirring frequently, to just below boiling point. Do not allow the coconut milk to boil or it will curdle. Lower the chicken pieces into the sauce, reheat it gently, then reduce the heat slightly and simmer the curry, uncovered, for 15 minutes. Continue to cook, uncovered, over very gentle heat, for a further 40 minutes or until the chicken is tender and the sauce has thickened.

Strain the lemon juice into the curry. Stir well to blend all the ingredients and coat the pieces of chicken thoroughly in the sauce. Arrange the curry in a warmed serving dish and serve immediately.

Note: Chicken thighs or 4 chicken portions may be used for this recipe and this will save having to cut up the whole chicken – a task which may be difficult if you do not have a meat cleaver or a sharp knife.

Gule Kambing

Spicy mutton curry

(Illustrated on page 95)
Indonesian curries have the basic spices added towards the end of the cooking
process rather than at the beginning as for Indian curries.
Serve hot with plain boiled rice and Sambal Ulek (page 93) if you are feeling
adventurous!

SERVES 4 · PREPARATION TIME 15–20 MINUTES · COOKING TIME 1½ HOURS

675 g/1½ lb lean boneless lamb or mutton
100 g/4 oz desiccated coconut (1⅓ cups
  shredded coconut)
3 tablespoons oil
4 cloves
2·5-cm/1-in stick cinnamon
pinch of ground nutmeg
2 teaspoons ground coriander
½ teaspoon ground cumin
2 medium onions
small piece fresh root ginger
2 cloves garlic

¾ teaspoon turmeric
chilli powder to taste
salt to taste
25 g/1 oz (¼ cup) macadamia nuts
1 stalk lemon grass or thinly pared rind
  of ½ lemon
small pinch loas powder – optional
4 curry leaves
2 tomatoes
750 ml/1¼ pints (3 cups) thick coconut
  milk (page 119)

Trim any excess fat from the lamb and cut it into 2·5-cm/1-in cubes. Dry-roast the coconut in a heavy-based frying pan (skillet) over low heat. Stir continuously until it is golden brown, and set aside. Heat 1 tablespoon of the oil in the same pan and fry the cloves, cinnamon, nutmeg, ground coriander and cumin for a minute then remove and set them aside.

Roughly chop the onions and ginger, then mix with the garlic, turmeric, chilli powder, salt, nuts, lemon grass, laos powder and the remaining oil. Grind all these ingredients to a smooth paste and fry it in a heavy-based saucepan until the oil has separated out and it is browned. Add the coconut, curry leaves and meat. Stir-fry until the meat is well browned and thoroughly coated in the spice mixture.

Peel and chop the tomatoes, add them to the meat and fry until they are reduced to a pulp. Add the coconut milk, stirring, and reduce the heat. Allow the sauce to simmer uncovered for 1 hour until the meat is tender. Finally add the fried spices, stir well and cook for a further 10–15 minutes.

Sambal Ulek

Chilli hot paste

This is really very hot, so beware! For those who are unaccustomed to such a taste it is best eaten in very small quantities along with plain boiled rice and other dishes. I would suggest that it is not tried on its own.
It can also be used to flavour various dishes to give that extra kick. It will keep well for several weeks in an airtight jar in the refrigerator.

PREPARATION TIME 5 MINUTES

15 fresh or dried red chillies (chili peppers)
1 teaspoon salt

150 ml/¼ pint vinegar or tamarind juice (page 119)

Remove the stalks from fresh red chillies or grind the dried chillies to a powder. Place the chillies, salt and vinegar or tamarind juice in a liquidiser and blend them to a smooth purée. Store in airtight jars in the refrigerator.

Nasi Gurih

Spicy coconut-flavoured rice

On festive occasions a variety of flavoured rice dishes are served instead of plain boiled rice. Here is a typical one.

SERVES 4 · PREPARATION TIME 15 MINUTES · COOKING TIME 30 MINUTES

450 g/1 lb (2 cups) long-grain rice
1 litre/1¾ (4¼ cups) pints thin coconut milk (page 119)
1 stalk lemon grass
pinch of ground nutmeg

pinch of ground mace
1–2 cloves
2–3 curry leaves
salt to taste
½ teaspoon freshly ground black pepper

Thoroughly rinse and drain the rice, then leave it to soak in fresh water for 10 minutes. Drain well. Mix the coconut milk, lemon grass, spices and curry leaves together in a large pan. Add the salt and pepper and bring it to the boil, then reduce the heat to its lowest setting and add the rice.

Stir well, cover and cook over low heat for 20 minutes, or until the rice is tender and the coconut milk has been absorbed. Fork up the rice, cook for another few minutes and serve immediately.

Sajur Lemeng
White vegetable curry

(Illustrated on opposite page)
This vegetable curry includes both prawns and shrimp paste, ingredients
without which no Indonesian dish is really complete. Serve with plain boiled
rice.

SERVES 4 · PREPARATION TIME 25 MINUTES · COOKING TIME 30-40 MINUTES

450 g/1 lb mixed vegetables in season,
  for example, marrow (summer
  squash), aubergines (egg plant),
  French beans or potatoes
1 medium onion
1 clove garlic
3–4 macadamia nuts
½ teaspoon shrimp paste
2 teaspoons ground coriander

½ teaspoon chilli powder
2 tablespoons oil
salt to taste
100 g/4 oz (¼ lb) peeled prawns
300 ml/½ pint (1¼ cups) thick coconut
  milk (page 119)
50 g/2 oz desiccated coconut (⅔ cup
  shredded coconut)

Prepare the vegetables and cut them all into thin strips. Roughly chop the
onion then grind it to a paste with the garlic, nuts, shrimp paste, coriander
powder, chilli powder and a little of the oil. Heat the remaining oil, add the
ground onion mixture and stir-fry until the mixture is well browned and the
oil starts to separate out. Add the salt and cook it for a few minutes. Stir in the
prawns, prepared vegetables and thick coconut milk. Moisten the desiccated
coconut with a little water and add it to the pan. Stir well and leave to simmer
gently until the vegetables are cooked and the sauce has thickened.

Clockwise from top right: Sajur Lemeng, Bawang Goreng (page 98) and
Gule Kambing (page 92)

Pacari

Spicy pineapple and coconut curry

(Illustrated on the back cover)
*Pacari consists of juicy pineapple cooked in a subtly spicy sauce with rich
coconut milk to give an unusually delicious and piquant dish.
Serve with plain boiled rice and Pisang Goreng (page 98).*

SERVES 4 · PREPARATION TIME 30 MINUTES · COOKING TIME 25–30 MINUTES

1 small ripe pineapple	1 teaspoon cumin seeds
1 small onion	2 teaspoons ground coriander
1 tablespoon oil	salt to taste
1 clove garlic, crushed	chilli powder to taste
2 green cardamoms	250 ml/8 fl oz (1½ cups) thick coconut
2 cloves	milk (page 119)
2·5-cm/1-in stick cinnamon	

Peel the pineapple, remove the leaves and cut it lengthways into quarters.
Remove and discard the central core, then cut it into bite-sized pieces. Chop
the onion. Heat the oil, add the onion, garlic and the whole spices and stir-fry
to a golden colour. Add the ground coriander, salt and chilli powder and stir-
fry for another few minutes to cook the spices. Reduce the heat, add the
pineapple pieces and stir well to coat them with the spice mixture. Finally, stir
in the coconut milk and simmer, uncovered, for 3–4 minutes until the
pineapple is just tender.

Note: If fresh pineapple is not available use canned pineapple chunks in
natural juice. Drain and discard the juice, then cook as above.

Clockwise from the top: Colombo de Poulet (page 105), Aaloo Talkari
(page 111), Crab Pullao (page 102) and Salade de Concombres (page 110)

Bawang Goreng
Deep fried onion rings

(Illustrated on page 95)
Indonesians are very fond of having a selection of side dishes with their meal.
Deep-fried onion rings are used as a garnish as well as to add flavour to many
dishes. Dried onion flakes instead of fresh onions may also be deep fried.

SERVES 4 · PREPARATION TIME 15 MINUTES · COOKING TIME 25 MINUTES

3 large onions   oil for deep frying

Peel and slice the onions very thinly taking care that the slices are of a uniform
thinness so that they cook evenly.
  Heat the oil for deep frying to 180 C/350 F. Sprinkle the onion slices into the
oil a few at a time and, as soon as they turn darkish brown, quickly scoop them
out and drain them thoroughly on absorbent kitchen paper. When quite cold
these onion rings may be stored in airtight containers for up to a week.

Pisang Goreng
Crisp fried bananas

Fried bananas are usually served as an accompaniment to curry and rice.
They are quick and easy to prepare and should be served immediately after they
are cooked.

SERVES 4 · PREPARATION TIME 3 MINUTES · COOKING TIME 8–10 MINUTES

4 medium, firm bananas   a little salt
oil for shallow frying

Cut the bananas in half lengthwise. Heat the oil in a large frying pan (skillet),
add the bananas and fry them until they are golden brown on the underside.
Turn them over very carefully – they break easily when hot – and fry until
golden on both sides. Serve sprinkled with salt.

Sambal Goreng Udang Asam
Piquant fried prawn sambal

Another dish which is considered a classic accompaniment to rice and curry, this sambal is made using small prawns or shrimps and is fairly economical.

SERVES 4 · PREPARATION TIME 15–20 MINUTES · COOKING TIME 20–25 MINUTES

350 g/12 oz ($\frac{3}{4}$ lb) peeled prawns
1 stalk lemon grass or thinly pared rind
 of $\frac{1}{2}$ lemon
1 medium onion
small piece fresh root ginger
1 clove garlic, crushed

2 tablespoons oil
1 teaspoon Sambal Ulek (page 93) or
 chilli powder
3 tablespoons tamarind juice (page 119)
salt to taste
sugar to taste

Roughly chop the prawns and chop the lemon grass. Finely chop the onion and ginger and mix them with the garlic. Heat the oil in a frying pan (skillet), add the onion mixture and stir-fry until the onion turns golden brown. Add the Sambal Ulek or chilli powder together with the lemon grass and continue to stir-fry for a few seconds. Stir in the prawns and cook them, stirring constantly, until they are thoroughly heated – about 5 minutes.

Add the tamarind juice and stir-fry until the sauce thickens and the oil separates out. Stir in the salt and sugar and mix well, then cook for a few seconds before serving hot.

West Indies

The West Indies in the Caribbean comprises a group of islands with beautiful sandy beaches, lush green vegetation and mountains covered in rain forests, stocked with flamboyant birds and butterflies. With plenty of rivers and a tremendous coastline, fishing is not really a sport but an important source of food.

When slavery was abolished in 1834 many of the free Africans left the plantations of Trinidad. They were replaced in 1845 by a labour force from East India, who brought with them the skills of their farming and cattle-breeding backgrounds, introducing rice cultivation, new methods of irrigation and a wide variety of foods suitable for growing in the islands. Most important of all, they also brought their curry spices.

Today curries are an accepted form of the local diet. Great use is made of coconut milk and coconut oil in cooking. Meat and poultry are popular, for although many Trinidadians are Hindus they are not necessarily vegetarians. In East India where most of them originally came from the staple diet is rice and fish.

Carnival time is a great excuse for celebration, and in Trinidad this means another occasion for eating, for in these carefree islands good food goes hand in hand with enjoyment of the unhurried, timeless days.

Caribbean Prawn Curry

To my mind, there is nothing better than large prawns cooked in fresh lime or lemon juice with a lot of spices. This prawn curry from Trinidad is similar to that cooked in India.
Serve it with Chapatis (page 122) and Mango Chutney (page 110).

SERVES 4 · PREPARATION TIME 15–20 MINUTES · COOKING TIME 40–45 MINUTES

2 medium onions	6–8 black peppercorns
small piece fresh root ginger	dried bay leaf
1 clove garlic	2–3 tablespoons oil
4 ripe tomatoes	1 tablespoon lemon juice
1 teaspoon coriander seeds	salt to taste
1 teaspoon cumin seeds	chilli powder to taste
1 teaspoon mustard seeds	450 g/1 lb peeled king prawns

Finely chop the onions, ginger, garlic and tomatoes. Grind the coriander, cumin and mustard seeds, peppercorns and bay leaf together to a fine powder. Heat the oil in a heavy-based saucepan, add the onion and stir-fry until golden brown. Add the ginger, garlic and ground spices and continue to cook for another few minutes before adding the chopped tomatoes and lemon juice. Season the curry to taste with the salt and chilli powder. Stir well, reduce the heat and cover the pan with a tight-fitting lid. Cook, stirring occasionally, until the tomatoes are reduced to a pulp. Add a little water if the sauce begins to stick to the pan.

Finally add the prawns, stir them in well to coat them in the sauce, then re-cover the pan and cook for another 5–10 minutes until the prawns are thoroughly heated. Transfer the curry to a warmed serving dish and serve immediately.

St. Kitts Curry Powder

There are two varieties of curry powder found in Martinique and Guadeloupe. One is the Poudre de Colombo (page 104), and the other is this one, which can also be found commercially prepared and sold on market stalls. Unless this powder is going to be used frequently, it is advisable to make up small quantities which can be used up quickly before the aroma and flavour of the ground spices is lost.

MAKES 225 G/8 OZ · PREPARATION TIME 15 MINUTES

25 g/1 oz (¼ cup) coriander seeds
25 g/1 oz (¼ cup) black peppercorns
50 g/2 oz (½ cup) white cumin seeds
1 tablespoon cloves
1 tablespoon poppy seeds

1 tablespoon brown mustard seeds
25 g/1 oz (4 tablespoons) ground
  Jamaican ginger
50 g/2 oz (½ cup) ground turmeric

Mix the coriander seeds, black peppercorns, white cumin seeds, cloves, poppy seeds and the mustard seeds in a heavy-based frying pan (skillet). Stirring continuously, dry roast the spices over low heat until they begin to pop and emit a delicate aroma. Remove the spices from the pan to prevent further cooking. Grind all the roasted spices to a fine powder. To achieve this, keep sieving the ground spices and repeatedly grinding the remaining coarse particles. Store in an air-tight jar for up to a month.

Crab Pullao

(Illustrated on page 96)
Crabs are in plentiful supply in the Caribbean so it is not surprising that they are widely used in the curries from this region.

SERVES 4 · PREPARATION TIME 20 MINUTES · COOKING TIME 35–40 MINUTES

450 g/1 lb (2 cups) long-grain rice
450 g/1 lb cooked crabmeat
3–4 tablespoons lemon juice
2 tablespoons oil
1 large onion
1 clove garlic

1 green chilli (chili pepper)
1 tablespoon St. Kitts Curry Powder
  (page 102)
750 ml/1¼ pints (3 cups) thin coconut
  milk (page 119)
salt and pepper to taste

Rinse the rice then soak it in fresh water for 15–20 minutes. Cut the crabmeat into bite-sized pieces, mix it with the lemon juice, then set it aside for 10–15 minutes.

Heat the oil in a large heavy-based saucepan. Finely chop the onion and garlic. Remove the stalk and seeds from the chilli and chop it finely. Stir-fry the onion and garlic with the chilli until soft and lightly browned. Add the curry powder and stir-fry for a few minutes without allowing the onions to overcook.

Throughly drain the rice and add it to the onions. Stir-fry for a few minutes to coat the rice evenly with the spices. Carefully add the thin coconut milk and salt and pepper. Stir well, reduce the heat and cover the pan with a tight-fitting lid. Cook for 15–20 minutes until the rice is almost cooked. Add the marinated crab and lemon juice, lightly mixing it into the rice with a fork. Do not use a spoon as the rice will become mushy. Replace the lid and cook for a further 3–5 minutes until all the moisture has been absorbed and the crabmeat is heated through.

Saffron Chicken

The unique flavour of this dish is enhanced by the subtle taste and aroma of saffron.
Serve with plain boiled rice.

SERVES 4 · PREPARATION TIME 15 MINUTES · COOKING TIME 1¼ HOURS

1 (1-kg/2½lb) chicken
2 large onions
small piece fresh root ginger
1 fresh red or green chilli (chili pepper)
small pinch saffron
3 tablespoons oil

1 tablespoon St. Kitts Curry Powder
  (page 102)
salt and pepper to taste
300 ml/½ pint (1¼ cups) thin coconut milk
  (page 119)

Cut the chicken into eight pieces. Finely chop the onions and ginger. Remove the stalk and seeds from the chilli and chop it finely. Infuse the saffron in a teaspoon of water.

Heat the oil in a heavy-based saucepan and fry the chicken in it until it is golden brown. Drain on absorbent kitchen paper. Stir-fry the onion and ginger in the remaining oil until golden brown. Add the saffron, curry powder, chilli, salt and pepper, stir-fry for a minute then stir in the thin coconut milk and return the chicken to the pan. Heat through, then cover closely and reduce the heat. Simmer the chicken until tender – about 45 minutes.

Poudre de Colombo

This curry paste is best made immediately before use, or in a large quantity for freezing. Freeze in an ice-cube tray and then transfer it to a freezer bag. In this way, one or two cubes at a time can be used straight out of the freezer.

PREPARATION TIME 10 MINUTES

2 cloves garlic, crushed
1 fresh hot red pepper (chili pepper)
1 teaspoon coriander seeds

1 teaspoon mustard seeds
pinch of turmeric

If the garlic cloves are very large then use only one. Remove the stalk and seeds from the red pepper and mix it with the other ingredients. Grind them to a smooth paste. This quantity is approximately enough for a dish to serve 6–8 people. If the paste is to be frozen, wrap it in several sealed bags to prevent the flavour escaping.

Riz Creole

This is an unusual and very successful method of cooking rice.

SERVES 4 · PREPARATION TIME 10 MINUTES · COOKING TIME 25 MINUTES

225 g/8 oz (1 cup) long-grain rice
600 ml/1 pint (2½ cups) water

1 teaspoon salt

Rinse the rice in several changes of water. Place the rice, water and salt in a saucepan, bring it to the boil, then cover the pan with a tight-fitting lid and simmer the rice until all the moisture has been absorbed – about 15–20 minutes. Remove from the heat and quickly rinse the rice in cold water. Replace the damp rice in the pan, and dry it over very low heat until it is heated through. Serve immediately.

Colombo de Poulet
Chicken curry

(Illustrated on page 96)
West Indian curries will often include white or red wine, as well as Madeira,
sherry or – in certain cases – even rum. Traditionally, this dish is served with
Riz Creole (page 104).

SERVES 4 · PREPARATION TIME 30 MINUTES · COOKING TIME 1¾ HOURS

1 (1·25-kg/2½-lb) chicken
1 large onion
1 clove garlic
1 small green mango
100 g/4 oz (¼ lb) pumpkin
100 g/4 oz (¼ lb) green unripe papaya –
 optional
100 g/4 oz (¼ lb) aubergine (eggplant)
100 g/4 oz (¼ lb) dasheen or yams
1 fresh hot red pepper (chili pepper)

2 tablespoons coconut or ground-nut oil
1 tablespoon Poudre de Colombo
 (page 104)
1 tablespoon tamarind juice (page 119)
175 ml/6 fl oz (¾ cup) dry white wine or
 thick coconut milk (page 119)
salt to taste
1 teaspoon fresh lime juice
1 tablespoon dry Madeira or rum

Skin the chicken and remove all the meat from the carcass, cutting it into approximately 8 pieces. Place the carcass in a large saucepan, cover with water and bring it to the boil. Reduce the heat and cover the pan, then simmer for 1 hour. Strain the stock and simmer uncovered until reduced by approximately half.

Finely chop the onion and crush the garlic. Peel and coarsely grate or chop the mango, peel and thickly slice the pumpkin, papaya (if used), aubergine and dasheen or yams. Remove the stalk and seeds from the hot red pepper and chop it finely. Wash your hands thoroughly after handling the pepper as its juices will cause severe irritation to the eyes and skin.

Heat the oil in a heavy-based frying pan (skillet), add the chicken and cook gently, turning once, until golden brown on both sides. Drain carefully and transfer the chicken pieces to an ovenproof casserole, preferably earthenware. Add the onion to the pan and fry until golden in colour, taking care not to brown it too much. Add the garlic and the Poudre de Colombo and cook over gentle heat, stirring frequently, for 3–4 minutes. Add to the chicken together with the tamaraind juice, wine or coconut milk and 175 ml/6 fl oz (¾ cup) of the stock. Stir well to mix all the ingredients, add the salt, cover the dish and cook in a moderate oven (160 C, 325 F, Gas 3) for 1¾ hours until the chicken and the vegetables are tender. Stir in the lime juice and the Madeira or rum just before serving.

Martinique Lamb Curry

This exciting lamb curry is an interesting combination of Eastern and Western influence. Although it is generally believed that wine and citrus fruits do not marry well, in this instance the combination of the two flavours is most successful.

SERVES 4 · PREPARATION TIME 30 MINUTES · COOKING TIME 1¾ HOURS

675 g/1½ lb lean boneless leg of lamb
1 large onion
1 clove garlic
1 small raw green mango
225 g/8 oz (½ lb) small new potatoes
100 g/4 oz (¼ lb) pumpkin
225 g/8 oz baby courgettes
   (½ lb zucchini)

2 tablespoons oil
2 teaspoons tamarind juice (page 119)
1 tablespoon St. Kitts Curry Powder
   (page 102)
300 ml/½ pint (1¼ cups) dry white wine
salt and pepper to taste
1 tablespoon dark rum
squeeze of lime or lemon juice

Cut the lamb into 2·5-cm/1-in cubes. Finely chop the onion and garlic. Peel and chop the mango and scrape the new potatoes. Peel the pumpkin and cut it into small pieces. Slice the courgettes.

Heat the oil, add the lamb and stir-fry over medium heat until well browned. Drain and set aside. Add the onion and fry until pale golden. Add the garlic, tamarind juice, chopped mango and curry powder. Stir-fry for another few minutes, making sure that the curry powder does not burn. Return the meat to the pan and stir in the wine. Stir well, reduce the heat, cover and gently simmer the curry for about 1 hour until the lamb is almost tender.

Add the vegetables and seasoning. Stir well, cover and simmer for a further 20–30 minutes until the vegetables are tender. Lastly add the rum and lime or lemon juice, stir well and cook for 3–4 minutes.

Trinidad Beef Curry

Curry has become an important part of the daily diet of the local people from this region. A few variations have evolved from the original concept of curry introduced by the immigrant workers from India.
Serve with plain boiled rice and Mango chutney (page 110).

SERVES 4 · PREPARATION TIME 20 MINUTES · COOKING TIME 1½ HOURS

675 g/1½ lb lean braising steak (chuck
    steak)
2 large onions
2·5-cm/1-in piece fresh root ginger
2–3 cloves garlic
1–2 green chillies (chili peppers) –
    optional

3 tablespoons oil
2 tablespoons St. Kitts Curry Powder
    (page 102)
salt and pepper to taste
600 ml/1 pint (2½ cups) thin coconut
    milk (page 119)

Rinse the meat, trim off any excess fat and cut it into small cubes. Finely chop the onions, ginger and garlic. Remove the stalk and seeds from the chillies (if used) and chop them finely.

Heat the oil in a heavy-based pan. Add the chopped ingredients and stir-fry until pale golden in colour. Add the curry powder and continue to cook for another 5 minutes, taking care not to burn the curry spices. Add the meat and, stirring continuously, cook until it is well browned and thoroughly coated in the onion and spice mixture. Add the seasoning and stir well.

Pour in the coconut milk, stir well and heat through, then reduce the heat. Cover the pan and cook gently for 1¼ hours until the meat is tender.

Colombo de Giraumon

Pumpkin curry

*Many small oriental and West Indian shops now sell the more unusual
vegetables, like calabaza (West Indian pumpkin) but if this is not available,
then use ordinary yellow pumpkin instead.
Serve with Chapatis (page 122).*

SERVES 4 · PREPARATION TIME 15–20 MINUTES · COOKING TIME 25–30 MINUTES

450 g/1 lb calabaza or pumpkin
1 medium onion
1 clove garlic
2 ripe tomatoes
50 g/2 oz streaky bacon (3 bacon slices)
2 tablespoons oil

1 teaspoon St. Kitts Curry Powder
(page 102)
salt to taste
chilli powder to taste
1–2 cloves
a squeeze of lemon juice

Peel and cut the pumpkin into 2·5-cm/1-in cubes. Finely slice the onion, crush
the garlic and chop the tomatoes. Remove and discard the rind from the bacon,
then roughly chop it.

Heat the bacon in a heavy-based frying pan (skillet) and stir-fry over low
heat until the fat runs and the bacon is crisp. Remove and drain it on absorbent
kitchen paper. Add the oil to the bacon fat remaining in the pan, then add the
onion and stir-fry to golden brown. Add the garlic and curry powder, then
season to taste with the salt and chilli powder. Add the cloves and lemon juice
and stir-fry for a few seconds before adding the pumpkin and tomatoes. Stir
well, reduce the heat and cook, stirring frequently, for about 15–20 minutes
until the pumpkin and tomatoes are tender. They should be quite pulpy and
care must be taken to prevent the mixture from sticking to the pan. Stir it well
off the bottom of the pan and add a few drops of water if necessary. Transfer
the curry to a warmed serving dish and serve immediately.

Note: When making a curry and its accompaniments it is important, as with
any meal, to remember to time the preparation of each dish. If this curry is to be
served with Chapatis, make the dough in advance. At the end of the cooking
time, roll out and cook the chapatis. Transfer them to a covered serving dish and
keep them warm until the rest of the meal is served.

Tomatoes and Okra

*Ladyfingers or okra have always been my favourite vegetable. If fresh ones are
out of season use canned ones, though they are not nearly as tasty as
the fresh vegetable.
Serve together with plain boiled rice as an accompaniment
to meat or poultry curries.*

SERVES 4 · PREPARATION TIME 20 MINUTES · COOKING TIME 20–25 MINUTES

450 g/1 lb tender okra (ladyfingers)	2 ripe tomatoes
2 medium onions	2 tablespoons oil
1 green chilli (chili pepper)	1 clove garlic, crushed
salt to taste	

Wash and dry the okra on absorbent kitchen paper then trim off the stalk
ends. Thinly slice the onions. Remove the stalk and seeds from the chilli and
chop it finely. Roughly chop the tomatoes.

Heat the oil, add the okra and stir-fry until golden brown. Drain and set
aside. This should prevent them from becoming slimy on further cooking. Add
the onion to the remaining oil and fry it until golden brown. Add the garlic,
chilli and salt. Stir-fry for a few minutes until all the moisture has evaporated,
then return the okra to the pan with the tomatoes and cook for another 4–5
minutes, stirring occasionally.

Plantain or Cassava Chips

*Cassava or plantain (green cooking banana) chips are as popular in the curry-
eating world as potato chips are in the West. These can be served with drinks or
as an accompaniment to a meal.*

SERVES 4–6 · PREPARATION TIME 40 MINUTES · COOKING TIME 15 MINUTES

4 cassava root or green bananas	salt to taste
oil for deep frying	chilli powder to taste

Peel the cassava root or bananas and slice them as thinly as possible. Soak them
in ice-cold water for about 30 minutes so as to extract any excess starch.

Drain the slices thoroughly and pat them dry on absorbent kitchen paper.
Heat the oil to 180 C/350 F and cook the dried slices of cassava or green banana
a few at a time until golden brown. Do not over-brown them as they become
bitter. Drain on absorbent kitchen paper and sprinkle with salt and chilli
powder to taste. They can be stored in an airtight container for a few days.

Salade de Concombres
Cucumber Salad

(Illustrated on page 96)
This cucumber salad is one of the most crunchy and refreshing side dishes to serve with a curry.

SERVES 4 · PREPARATION TIME 30 MINUTES

1 small cucumber
½ teaspoon salt
1 clove garlic

1 green chilli (chili pepper)
1 tablespoon lemon juice

Peel the cucumber. Cut it lengthwise into quarters then into large chunks. Place these in a strainer and sprinkle them with the salt. Leave the cucumber to stand for 10–15 minutes to drain away any excess moisture.

Crush the garlic. Remove the stalk and seeds from the chilli and chop it finely. Strain the lemon juice. Drain the cucumber, rinse it in cold water, then place it in a serving bowl with the rest of the ingredients. Toss well and serve lightly chilled.

Mango Chutney

The word 'chutney' in the Indian language literally means to 'lick something in small quantities' – this is very appropriate as most chutneys are chilli hot and should only be eaten in small quantities. Unripened mangoes – that king of fruits – or papayas should be used for this chutney.

SERVES 6 · PREPARATION TIME 15 MINUTES · COOKING TIME 15 MINUTES

1 medium-sized unripe mango
1 small onion
1 clove garlic
2·5-cm/1-in piece fresh root ginger
1 green chilli (chili pepper)

100 g/4 oz (¾ cup) green raisins or
  sultanas (seedless white raisins)
salt to taste
300 ml/½ pint (1¼ cups) vinegar
225 g/8 oz (1 cup) brown sugar (coffee
  sugar)

Peel and finely chop the mango, onion, garlic and ginger. Mix all the ingredients together in a heavy-based saucepan and cook, stirring frequently, over gentle heat until all the moisture has evaporated (about 15 minutes) and the chutney has thickened. Cool and store in an airtight container for up to a week.

Aaloo Talkari

New potato and mango chutney

(Illustrated on page 96)
*Fenugreek seeds can impart a very bitter and unpleasant taste if used whole, but
their flavour is quite unique. This recipe uses them to best advantage by frying
them in coconut oil to extract all the flavour and then discarding the actual
seeds. Buy the smallest potatoes available for this chutney.
Serve as an accompaniment to meat or poultry curries or with Chapatis
(page 122).*

SERVES 4 · PREPARATION TIME 5–10 MINUTES · COOKING TIME 20–30 MINUTES

450 g/1 lb small new potatoes
1 raw green mango
1 clove garlic
2 tablespoons coconut oil
2 teaspoons fenugreek seeds

1 tablespoon St. Kitts Curry Powder
(page 102)
salt to taste
150 ml/¼ pint (⅔ cup) water

Scrape and wash the potatoes then soak them in cold water for 5–10 minutes.
Peel the firm green skin off the mango and cut the flesh into thin slices.
Roughly chop the garlic.

Heat the oil, add the fenugreek seeds and the garlic and fry, stirring
continuously, until the seeds are well browned. Carefully remove all the seeds
and garlic from the pan and discard these. Add the curry powder to the hot oil,
standing well back in case it splutters, and cook it for 3–4 minutes, stirring
continuously.

Stir in the potatoes, mango slices and salt. Finally add the water. Mix
thoroughly, cover the pan and cook over low heat for approximately 15
minutes until the potatoes are tender and most of the moisture has evaporated.
Check that the mixture does not stick to the pan, then coarsely mash the
chutney with a fork before serving.

East Africa

When an Indian from Kenya, Uganda or Tanzania is asked where he comes from, the answer is usually East Africa, since most of them have at some time or another lived in all three countries.

The Indian people who settled in Kenya, Uganda and Tanzania over a century ago came mainly from Gujarat in the West and Punjab in the North of India, and they brought with them their respective food preferences and customs. The Gujaratis have a strong vegetarian tradition and their diet consists of a wide variety of vegetables and pulses, sprouted and lightly fried or eaten raw with the addition of herbs and spices. The Punjabis, on the other hand, are predominantly non-vegetarians and enjoy a good mixed diet, rich in proteins and all the other essential ingredients.

Even though the Asian community has lived in East Africa for at least two or three generations, their diet has undergone very little change. Socially, they have never mixed with their African neighbours, and have not adopted any of the native African dishes. The curries, therefore, are very similar to those found in the regions of India from which the two communities originally came.

Dilruba Chops

Baked lamb chops

Lamb chops are best marinated in yogurt and spices and cooked slowly. The marinade helps to tenderise the meat and keeps it moist and succulent during the slow cooking.
Serve with Chapatis (page 122) or Clove Rice (page 113).

SERVES 4 · PREPARATION TIME 4¼ HOURS · COOKING TIME 1¼ HOURS

1 kg/2 lb lamb chops
2 green chillies (chili peppers)
600 ml/1 pint (2½ cups) natural yogurt
1 tablespoon ground coriander
2 teaspoons ground cumin

salt to taste
2 teaspoons garam masala (page 119)
4 tablespoons concentrated tomato purée (tomato paste)
2 tablespoons chopped coriander leaves

Rinse and dry the chops on absorbent kitchen paper. Place them in an ovenproof dish. Remove the stalks and seeds from the green chillies and chop them finely then mix with the yogurt and all the remaining ingredients. Pour over the chops, turning them to ensure that they are thoroughly coated in the marinade. Leave for 4 hours, longer if possible, and turn the chops over once or twice during the marinating time.

Cook the chops, in their marinade, in a moderate oven (160 c, 325 f, Gas 3) for 1–1¼ hours until tender. Baste occasionally with the yogurt mixture and serve them hot.

Clove Rice

This simple rice dish, flavoured delicately with cloves, is most refreshing.

SERVES 4 · PREPARATION TIME 30 MINUTES · COOKING TIME 30 MINUTES

450 g/1 lb (2 cups) long-grain rice
1 tablespoon ghee (page 118)

2–3 cloves
about 1·15 litres/2 pints (5 cups) water

Rinse the rice, then soak it in fresh water for 20–30 minutes. Heat the ghee in a saucepan, add the cloves and fry them for 2 minutes. Drain the rice thoroughly and add it to the cloves, stir-fry for a few minutes, then pour in enough water to come 2·5 cm/1 in over the top of rice. Bring to the boil, reduce the heat then cover with a tight-fitting lid and cook for 20–25 minutes until the rice is tender and all the water has been absorbed. Serve hot.

Methi Aaloo
Fenugreek leaves and potatoes

Fenugreek leaves can be bought either fresh or dried and both are delicious. Dried leaves should be soaked for at least 30 minutes before use. Small new potatoes are particularly good in this dish as their delicate flavour complements the fenugreek leaves.
Serve as an accompaniment to meat and poultry curries.

SERVES 4 · PREPARATION TIME 20 MINUTES · COOKING TIME 30 MINUTES

225 g/8 oz ($\frac{1}{2}$ lb) fresh or 100 g/4 oz ($\frac{1}{4}$ lb) dried fenugreek leaves
225 g/8 oz ($\frac{1}{2}$ lb) small new potatoes
2 tablespoons oil
1 teaspoon ajwain seeds

salt to taste
chilli powder to taste
$\frac{1}{2}$ teaspoon turmeric
150 ml/$\frac{1}{4}$ pint ($\frac{2}{3}$ cup) water

Wash fresh fenugreek leaves and shake them dry. If dried ones are used, soak them for 30 minutes, then strain and rinse them before use. Roughly chop the prepared leaves and their stalks. Scrub or scrape the potatoes and cut them into quarters.

Heat the oil in a heavy-based saucepan, sprinkle the ajwain seeds in and cook them quickly until they pop, then add the salt, chilli powder and turmeric. Stir-fry for a few seconds before adding the fenugreek leaves and potatoes. Continue to stir-fry for 2–3 minutes to mix the ingredients thoroughly.

Pour in the water and bring it to the boil, then cover the pan and reduce the heat. Cook, stirring frequently, for 15 minutes until the potatoes are tender and all the excess moisture has evaporated. Transfer the vegetables to a warmed serving dish and serve immediately.

Dandal

Spicy cauliflower stalks

It is indeed a crime to throw away the tender green stalks which surround the base of the cauliflower. Cut into small pieces and cooked with fresh ginger, spices and tomatoes, they make a very interesting and delicious dish. The use of ajwain seeds imparts a very subtle aromatic flavour.
Serve with Dall (page 121), Chapatis (page 122) and yogurt.

SERVES 4 · PREPARATION TIME 25 MINUTES · COOKING TIME 35–40 MINUTES

tender green stalks trimmed from two cauliflowers	1 teaspoon ajwain seeds
	salt to taste
2 medium onions	chilli powder to taste
2·5-cm/1-in piece fresh root ginger	½ teaspoon turmeric
1 clove garlic	1 teaspoon ground coriander
3–4 ripe tomatoes	300 ml/½ pint (1¼ cups) water
2–3 tablespoons oil	1 teaspoon dried mango powder

Thoroughly wash the cauliflower stalks and cut them into small pieces. Finely chop the onions, ginger, garlic and tomatoes. Heat the oil in a large frying pan (skillet). Sprinkle in the ajwain seeds and cook quickly until they pop – this should only take a few seconds. Stir in the onion, ginger and garlic and stir-fry until golden brown in colour. Add the salt, chilli powder, turmeric and ground coriander. Stir-fry for a few minutes then add the tomatoes.

Cook the vegetables, stirring them occasionally, until the tomatoes are soft, then stir in the cauliflower stalks. Continue cooking, still stirring frequently, for a further 3–5 minutes.

Pour in the water, mix well and bring to the boil. Reduce the heat, cover the pan and simmer the Dandal until the cauliflower stalks are tender and all the moisture has evaporated. Sprinkle the dried mango powder on top and, stirring continuously, cook for another few minutes. Spoon the mixture into a warmed serving dish and serve immediately.

Spicy Moong Dall
Spicy mung beans

The West has now realised the important role legumes play in the diet. Rich in protein, they make a useful meat substitute. Whole green moong dall are generally sold in shops as sprouted moong beans – so popular in Chinese cooking and for salads.
Serve with plain boiled rice or Chapatis (page 122).

SERVES 4 · PREPARATION TIME 15 MINUTES · COOKING TIME 45 MINUTES

150 g/5 oz ($\frac{1}{2}$ cup) whole moong dall
600 ml/1 pint (2$\frac{1}{2}$ cup) water
salt to taste
chilli powder to taste
$\frac{1}{2}$ teaspoon turmeric

2–3 ripe tomatoes
small piece fresh root ginger
1 teaspoon dried mango powder
$\frac{1}{2}$ teaspoon ground cumin
2–3 curry leaves

Thoroughly wash and rinse the dall. Drain and place them in a saucepan with the water, salt, chilli powder and turmeric. Bring to the boil, reduce the heat and cover the pan. Simmer the dall for approximately 40 minutes until they are tender but retain their shape. By now most of the water should have been absorbed.

Quarter the tomatoes, finely chop the ginger and stir into the dall together with the mango powder, cumin, and curry leaves. Stir well to mix all the ingredients. Cover and cook over low heat for another few minutes before serving.

Poori
Wholemeal deep fried bread

Crisply fried bread is very popular all over India, too, and can either be plain, or stuffed with a variety of mixtures. The dough is the same as that used to make chapatis but poori are smaller.

SERVES 4 · PREPARATION TIME 10 MINUTES · COOKING TIME 15 MINUTES

225 g/8 oz (2 cups) wholemeal
   flour

150 ml/$\frac{1}{4}$ pint ($\frac{2}{3}$ cup) water
oil for deep frying

Prepare the dough as for the Chapatis (page 122). Heat the oil for deep frying to 180 c/350 f. Meanwhile, break off small pieces of the dough and roll it out thinly to circles measuring 10 cm/4 in. in diameter. Avoid too much dry flour to roll out the dough as any excess may overcook and burn during frying.

Carefully lift the circles of dough into the hot oil and cook, turning them once, until the poori are puffed and brown. Use a fish slice to gently press the poori into the oil during cooking to make it puff up. Drain on absorbent kitchen paper and serve hot.

Aaloo Parathas

Potato-stuffed parathas

Stuffed parathas have always been regarded as being traditionally Punjabi. Normally eaten for breakfast or Sunday brunch with natural yogurt and butter, they are delicious when hot and crisp.

SERVES 4 · PREPARATION TIME 1 HOUR · COOKING TIME 40 MINUTES

450 g/1 lb (4 cups) wholemeal flour
300 ml/½ pint (1¼ cups) water
450 g/1 lb potatoes
1 medium onion
small piece fresh root ginger

1 teaspoon ajwain seeds
salt to taste
chilli powder to taste
½ teaspoon garam masala (page 119)
4 tablespoons oil

Prepare the dough as for Chapatis (page 122). Cook the unpeeled potatoes in boiling salted water for 25 minutes or until tender. Peel, mash and leave them to cool.

Finely chop the onion and ginger, add them to the potatoes together with all the remaining ingredients except the oil. Break off small pieces of the dough about the size of a large walnut and roll each into a circle measuring 10 cm/4 in in diameter. Spread about 1 tablespoon of the potato mixture on half the dough circles and dampen their edges. Place a second piece of dough on top and firmly press down around the edges to seal in the filling. Carefully roll out to give circles measuring 15 cm/6 in in diameter.

Heat the oil in a large frying pan (skillet), carefully lift the parathas into the pan and cook them, one at a time for a few seconds until small bubbles appear on top. Turn over, and cook them on the other side for a few seconds. Repeat this process once more and give a final turn until the paratha is crisp and golden. Serve hot with plain yogurt and butter.

Note: These freeze very well and may easily be reheated from frozen under a hot grill.

Basic Recipes

Paneer
Indian cheese

MAKES 225 G/8 OZ · PREPARATION TIME 14 HOURS

1·15 litres/2 pint (5 cups) full cream
milk

3 tablespoons lemon juice
muslin or cheesecloth for straining

Pour the milk into a heavy-based saucepan and bring it to the boil. Whisk in the strained lemon juice, then remove the pan from the heat and allow it to cool completely, whisking occasionally. This curdled milk is the cheese and the thin whey that separates off should be drained away. Strain the cheese through a clean muslin cloth. Tie it up and hang it overnight to drain (or strain the cheese through a muslin-lined sieve then leave to drain overnight).

The paneer can be used for sweetmeats and desserts, or pressed flat, cut in pieces and fried for use in curries and savoury snacks.

Ghee
Clarified butter

Many stores sell ghee packed in cans or in small plastic tubs, but it can also be made most successfully at home. For best results use unsalted butter, otherwise good quality salted butter. Melt 1 kg/2 lb (4 cups) butter over very low heat in a heavy-based saucepan. Leave it to simmer gently for 25–30 minutes. Most of the water will have evaporated by this time and a sediment will have settled at the bottom of the pan. Remove the pan from the heat and strain the contents carefully through a piece of muslin into a clean bowl. Discard the sediment and store the Ghee (clarified butter) in a covered container for up to 3 months.

Coconut Milk

The clear liquid inside the coconut is often mistaken for coconut milk but it is in fact coconut water – pierce two of the eyes and drain it into a jug. Use a hammer to crack the coconut open. Coconut *milk* is obtained by scraping the white flesh out of the coconut and squeezing out all the liquid. The first batch is thick coconut milk. Thin coconut milk is obtained by immersing the grated coconut flesh in warm water to cover and squeezing it out. This can be repeated 2–3 times before the grated coconut is discarded.

Ready-made coconut cream is sold in 225-g/8-oz packets and is dissolved in a little warm water to give coconut milk. Desiccated coconut (shredded coconut) may be soaked in warm water to cover, then squeezed out to obtain thin coconut milk.

Tamarind Juice

The green tamarind pods are dried to become dark brown and pulpy. They are then broken up, pressed into slabs and sold in packets. To make tamarind juice, break off a small piece of the slab about the size of a 5-cm/2-in cube and soak it for 15 minutes in enough warm water to cover it completely. Squeeze out the pods to release the soft pulp, then strain and reserve the juice, discarding the stones and any fibres.

Ready-made concentrated tamarind pulp is also available and should be diluted with eight times the amount of warm water before use.

Garam Masala

Good quality garam masala may be purchased from many shops, but it is best purchased in small quantities as the ground spices soon lose their flavour.

MAKES ABOUT 6–8 TABLESPOONS · PREPARATION TIME 10 MINUTES

3 tablespoons whole black peppercorns
2 tablespoons cumin seeds
5-cm/2-in stick cinnamon

2 tablespoons cloves
8 cardamoms
6 bay leaves

Grind all the ingredients together to form a very fine powder and store in an airtight jar.

Boiled Rice

There are many different varieties of rice grown and marketed and equally as many different methods of cooking it. Some wash rice first to rinse away excess starch; others prefer not to. Certain types of rice need prolonged soaking; others not at all. Perfectly boiled rice is difficult to achieve and the merit of the Indian bride-to-be is often judged on her ability to produce perfect, white fluffy rice. The ratio of water to rice is most important, the accepted ratio being one cup of rice to two cups of water. I find that this is not always ideal for pre-soaked rice as some moisture is absorbed during the pre-soaking, and the result is sticky. As a general rule, I recommend cooking it in water to a depth of 2·5 cm/1 in above the rice in the pan to produce perfect results.

SERVES 4 · PREPARATION TIME 40 MINUTES · COOKING TIME 20 MINUTES

275 g/10 oz (1¼ cups) Patna, Basmati or long-grain rice

about 750 ml/1¼ pints (3 cups) water
½ teaspoon salt

Rinse the rice, then drain and soak it in fresh water for at least 30 minutes. Drain the rice and place it in a saucepan with the water and salt. Bring to the boil, reduce the heat and cover the pan. Simmer very gently for about 20 minutes until the rice is tender and dry. Fluff it up with a fork before serving.

Zaffran Pullao
Pullao rice

(Illustrated on page 43)
Pullaos are traditional in Muslim homes, and my neighbours in Karachi used to prepare the most delicious saffron pullao using dried fruits instead of meat or poultry.
Serve as an accompaniment to meat or poultry curries.

SERVES 4 · PREPARATION TIME 45 MINUTES · COOKING TIME 25–30 MINUTES

450 g/1 lb (2 cups) Basmati rice
1 medium onion
2 tablespoons ghee (page 118)
¼ teaspoon black cumin seeds
2·5-cm/1-in stick cinnamon
1–2 black cardamoms
2–3 cloves

bay leaf
½ teaspoon saffron strands
50 g/2 oz (½ cup) slivered almonds
25 g/1 oz green raisins or sultanas
(3 tablespoons white raisins)
about 750 ml/1¼ pints (3 cups) water
1 teaspoon salt

Rinse the rice and soak it in fresh water for 30 minutes. Thinly slice the onion. Heat the ghee in a heavy-based saucepan, add the onion and all the spices except the saffron. Stir-fry until the onion turns golden brown. Add the almonds, raisins and well-drained rice and stir-fry for a further 5 minutes.

Soak the saffron in one tablespoon of water for a few minutes. Pour it over the rice together with enough water to cover to a depth of 2·5 cm/1 in. Add the salt, stir well and bring to the boil. Reduce the heat, cover the pan closely and cook slowly for about 20 minutes until the rice is tender and fluffy and the water is absorbed. Fluff up the rice with a fork and serve immediately.

Dall

Spiced lentils

Wherever Indian immigrants have settled, they have taken with them not only the curry spices but also a variety of lentils and other pulse. Dall, as these legumes are popularly known, are high in protein and a valuable addition to the vegetarian diet.

SERVES 4 · PREPARATION TIME 2¼ HOURS · COOKING TIME 25–30 MINUTES

225 g/8 oz (1 cup) Egyptian or green lentils	1 small onion, finely chopped
600 ml/1 pint (2½ cups) water	1 tablespoon ghee (page 118)
salt to taste	1 teaspoon cumin seeds
½ teaspoon turmeric	1–2 cloves
	1 clove garlic, crushed

Rinse the lentils thoroughly then soak them in fresh water for 2 hours. Drain and transfer them to a saucepan and add the water, salt and turmeric. Bring to the boil then reduce the heat, cover the pan and cook for approximately 20 minutes until the dall are tender and slightly mushy. Add the finely chopped onion, stir well and cook until the mixture has thickened.

Heat the ghee in a small frying pan (skillet), add the cumin seeds, cloves and crushed garlic. Stir-fry for a few minutes until the seeds pop and the garlic is golden brown. Pour this over the cooked dall, stir well and serve with plain boiled rice.

Chapatis
Unleavened wholemeal bread

(Illustrated on page 41)
All over northern, central and certain parts of the western region of India, the chapati is the staple diet. Traditionally chapatis are freshly prepared at each meal; however I find that, cooked, they freeze very well. There is no need to defrost the chapatis before reheating – simply place them under a hot grill for a few minutes.

MAKES 8–10 · PREPARATION TIME 45 MINUTES · COOKING TIME 30 MINUTES

225 g/8 oz (2 cups) wholemeal flour   150 ml/¼ pint (⅔ cup) water

Place the flour in a bowl, gradually stir in the water and knead thoroughly to give a smooth dough – it may be kneaded with the dough hook in a food mixer. Wrap the dough in cling film and leave it to rest for 15–20 minutes in the refrigerator.

Slowly heat a large heavy-based frying pan (skillet) or griddle (tava). Break off small pieces of dough about the size of a walnut. Shape them into smooth balls, then roll out on a floured surface into rounds measuring approximately 10 cm/4 in. in diameter. Carefully lift the dough into the pan or on to the griddle and then cook for a few seconds on one side. Turn the chapatis over and cook on the other side until small bubbles start appearing on the surface. Turn it back immediately and cook for a further few seconds so that the underneath is cooked. Gently press down the edges to ensure that they are cooked. Serve immediately, either plain or spread with a little ghee.

Parathas

Parathas are the most popular breads in India and they are freshly baked for each meal.

SERVES 4 · PREPARATION TIME 15 MINUTES · COOKING TIME 20 MINUTES

225 g/8 oz (2 cups) wholemeal flour   50 g/2 oz (¼ cup) ghee (page 118)
150 ml/¼ pint (⅔ cup) water

Mix the flour and water in a bowl and knead it to a smooth dough. Leave the dough to rest for 10–15 minutes. Break off small pieces of dough about the size of a walnut and roll them out into 10-cm/4-in rounds. Smear a little ghee over each, fold one-third towards the centre, spread more ghee on top then fold the other third over this. Fold the dough in the same way from the long side, so that you are left with a small square. Dip this square in a little flour and roll it out into a 10-cm/4-in square.

Heat a tava or heavy-based frying pan (skillet). Carefully cook the paratha for a few minutes, then turn it over and cook it on the other side. Smear some ghee on the top, turn it over and let it fry for a few seconds. Repeat the process once more, frying the paratha until it is crisp and browned. Serve immediately.

Naan

Unlike most Indian breads, naan is made with plain flour and bound into a pliable dough with natural yogurt.

SERVES 4 · PREPARATION TIME 2½ HOURS · COOKING TIME 10−12 MINUTES

275 g/10 oz plain flour (2½ cups all-purpose flour)
½ teaspoon baking powder
1 teaspoon salt
small pinch bicarbonate of soda (baking soda)

4 tablespoons natural yogurt
1 egg, lightly beaten
1 tablespoon oil
1 tablespoon poppy seeds

Sift the flour, baking powder, salt and bicarbonate of soda into a bowl. Lightly beat the yogurt and add it to the dry ingredients with the egg and oil. Knead the mixture into a fairly stiff dough, adding a little extra yogurt if necessary. Cover the dough with a clean damp cloth and leave it in a warm place for 2−3 hours, by which time it should almost have doubled in size. Knead the dough lightly then break off pieces about the size of a large plum and roll them out into 15-cm/6-in circles. Dampen one side of the naan and place them on a greased baking tray, dampened side down. Sprinkle a few poppy seeds on top and bake in a moderately hot oven (200 C, 400 F, Gas 6) for 10−12 minutes until small brown spots appear on the surface. Serve immediately as the naan tend to become a little rubbery when cold.

Glossary

Ajwain seeds Strong, spicy seeds with digestive properties. Similar in appearance to celery and thyme seeds.

Aniseeds Small, oval seeds, light green or brown in colour, with a distinct flavour which resembles liquorice. Used whole or ground and traditionally chewed after a meal to aid digestion.

Asafoetida A strong and aromatic spice obtained from the gum of a plant and for use in only the smallest quantities.

Calabaza pumpkin West Indian pumpkin, slightly oval with green flecked skin and golden-orange flesh. Substitute English or American pumpkin.

Cardamoms Black or green, both with strong digestive properties and used whole or ground in curries. Black cardamoms are larger than green ones.

Cassava root The root of the tropical cassava or manioc shrub.

Chana dall Chick peas or grams, dried or canned; the dried ones need prolonged soaking and cooking.

Chillies Green or red, originally from Mexico but now available all over the world. Fresh, dried or as chilli powder, they should always be used with care as they are very pungent and strong in flavour.

Cinnamon stick The bark of the cassia tree grown in Sri Lanka. The sticks are approximately 10 cm/4 in. in length with a strong aroma and flavour.

Coriander The whole plant is used in Indian and South East Asian cooking. The seeds are used whole or ground and the leaves and roots are chopped for use as a flavouring or garnish. The fresh leaves are also known as Chinese parsley.

Cumin seeds Small long seeds, white or black, with a refreshing flavour and aroma. Must not be confused with caraway seeds.

Curry leaves Small, dark green, shiny, aromatic leaves which should not be confused with bay leaves. Available fresh or dried.

Dall Pulses and dried beans.

Dasheen A root vegetable similar to yams but not as widely available.

Fenugreek Leaves or seeds are eaten. Squarish, dull yellow seeds with a bitter taste; use either whole or ground in small quantities.

Fish sauce Strong-flavoured, oily sauce which is an essential ingredient in South East Asian cooking. Available from specialist shops.

Garam masala A mixture of five or six spices ground together. Can be purchased ready ground or made at home (see page 119).

Ghee Clarified butter (see page 118).

Laos powder A delicate spice used in South East Asian cooking, difficult to obtain but not an essential ingredient.

Lemon grass Tall, aromatic grass, available in good supermarkets and specialist stores. Substitute thinly pared lemon rind.

Macadamia nuts Small, round, pale and buttery nuts. Sold shelled and roasted.

Mango powder Dried raw green mangoes, ground to make a sour powder.

Moong dall Mung beans, used whole or split, with or without their skins. Sprouted mung beans are known as bean sprouts.

Masoor dall Red lentils.

Nigella seeds Small black triangular seeds with a slightly peppery taste.

Plantain Cooking bananas – starchier and not as sweet as the eating variety.

Rampe leaves Difficult to obtain but used in Malaysian or Indonesian dishes.

Tamarind Sour pods from the tamarind tree; the pods are dried and pressed into blocks. Pieces may be soaked to make tamarind juice (page 119).

Urad dall Split black beans.

Yam Brown skinned vegetable with white or slightly yellow flesh. Readily available.

Index